DINOSAURS

THE GOOD, THE BAD, AND THE UGLY

DINOSAURS

THE GOOD, THE BAD, AND THE UGLY

By
Dougal Dixon

Consultant
David Lambert

A Dorling Kindersley Book

Dorling **DK** Kindersley

LONDON, NEW YORK, SYDNEY, DELHI,
PARIS, MUNICH, and JOHANNESBURG

Project Editor Steve Setford
Project Art Editor Peter Radcliffe
Senior Editor Fran Jones
Senior Art Editor Marcus James
Category Publisher Jayne Parsons
Managing Art Editor Jacquie Gulliver
Picture Researcher Sean Hunter
Production Erica Rosen
DTP Designers Matthew Ibbotson and Louise Paddick

First published in Great Britain in 2001 by
Dorling Kindersley Limited
80 Strand, London WC2R 0RL

2 4 6 8 10 9 7 5 3

The CIP Catalogue record for this
book is available
from the British Library

ISBN 0-7513-3080-9

Reproduced by Colourscan, Singapore
Printed and bound by L.E.G.O., Italy

See our complete
catalogue at
www.dk.com

CONTENTS

INTRODUCTION

Dinosaurs! We see their skeletons in museums, photographs of them in books, and images of them in films and on television. But what were these amazing creatures that have so caught our imagination? And how do we know so much about them?

The name dinosaur means "terrible lizard". These creatures were land-living reptiles that dominated life on Earth about 225 to 65 million years ago, during the Mesozoic Era. The Mesozoic is often referred to as "the Age of Reptiles". Scientists have divided this part of history into three periods of time – the Triassic, the Jurassic, and the Cretaceous. You'll learn more about the world during these periods as you read this book.

Nobody knew anything about dinosaurs until about 200 years ago. Ancient peoples saw dinosaur fossils in the rocks, but they did not

STEGOCERAS WAS A SMALL DINOSAUR THAT LIVED ABOUT 70 MILLION YEARS AGO, IN THE LATE CRETACEOUS. IT ATE FRUIT, LEAVES, AND INSECTS.

understand what they were. After all, if you knew nothing about dinosaurs and discovered a limb-bone that was as long as you are, what would you make of it – a giant or a dragon perhaps? The first remains to be studied properly were found in England in the early 19th century. Soon, discoveries were being made in mainland Europe and in North America as well. Since then, dinosaur remains have been found on every continent, with the first Antarctic discoveries occurring during the 1980s.

Over the past two centuries, palaeontologists (fossil experts) and other scientists have been drawing together all the evidence. Now we think we have a good idea of what dinosaurs were and how they lived. But new discoveries often turn established ideas on their heads. It's because we keep making new discoveries and finding new evidence that dinosaur science is so exciting.

For those of you who want to explore the subject in more detail, there are black Log On "bites" that appear throughout the book. These will direct you to some terrific websites where you can find out even more. Welcome to the ever-changing world of dinosaurs!

DINO SPOTTING

You stand in an ancient forest, with unfamiliar conifer trees towering over you, the ferny undergrowth tickling your legs, and strange insects buzzing around you in the heat. In front of you, in the shade of a tree, is an animal you have never seen before. It is about your size and it is standing on its hind legs. It is a dinosaur!

Plant- or meat-eater?
What kind of dinosaur is it? As you mentally flick through all your dinosaur books, some of the names come back to you. Meat-eating *Deinonychus* and *Ornitholestes*, plant-eating *Hypsilophodon* and *Stegoceras* – all are about the same size and walk on their hind legs. But is this one a gentle plant-eater or is it a fierce meat-eater? If it likes to nibble leaves, shoots, and other vegetation, it will not bother you; if it prefers a nice big juicy steak, you are in deep trouble! The dinosaur is staring at you, so you need to find out quickly. But first you will need to check out a few things.
1. How is it standing? All meat-eaters – the dinosaur group scientists call the theropods – walked on their hind legs, using their tails for balance. But that doesn't help us much, as the main group of plant-eaters – the ornithopods – also walked on their hind legs, just as the one in front of you is doing right now.
2. Look at its jaws and teeth. If it has long jaws and sharp, pointed teeth, it is a meat-eater. If it has short jaws, with a beak

WEIRD WORLD
SCIENTISTS THINK THAT THERE MAY HAVE BEEN 1,500 DIFFERENT DINOSAURS. TO DATE, WE KNOW ABOUT 300 OF THEM. SO, IF WE CAME FACE TO FACE WITH A DINOSAUR, THERE WOULD BE ONLY A ONE IN FIVE CHANCE THAT WE'D RECOGNIZE IT.

A SMALL IGUANODON IN A GLOOMY FOREST WOULD MAKE ANYONE STOP AND LOOK. AT FIRST GLANCE, HOWEVER, IT WOULD BE DIFFICULT TO TELL WHETHER THIS ANIMAL WERE DANGEROUS OR NOT.

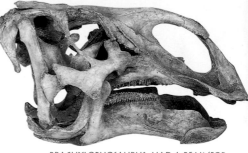

BRACHYLOPHOSAURUS HAD A BEAK (FOR
SNIPPING UP PLANTS), GRINDING TEETH
BEHIND, AND A STRONG JAW HINGE. IT HAD
CHEEK POUCHES AT THE SIDE, SO IT COULD
CHEW GREAT MOUTHFULS OF PLANTS.

at the front and cheeks at the
side, it is a plant-eater. But with
its head turned towards you, it
may be difficult to tell.
3. Count the fingers (if you're
close enough and brave
enough). Most two-footed
plant-eaters had five or four
fingers, whereas meat-eaters
usually had three or two, and
these had hooked claws.
4. The body size should be a
giveaway. Meat-eaters had very
slim bodies, helping them to
run fast, while plant-eaters had
larger, wider bodies, because
they needed a bigger digestive
system for the food they ate.
5. Can you see its colour? This
is not a reliable guide, but meat-
eaters were probably brightly
coloured, striped, or spotted like

LONG-NECKED, PLANT-EATING BAROSAURUS
DID NOT HAVE GRINDING TEETH. IT HAD
NO WAY OF CHEWING ITS FOOD, SO IT JUST
RAKED LEAFY TWIGS INTO ITS MOUTH AND
SWALLOWED THEM.

MEAT-EATING ALBERTOSAURUS HAD SHARP RIPPING TEETH, ALL DIFFERENT SIZES AND SERRATED LIKE STEAK KNIVES. THE JAW IS HINGED FOR CHOMPING FOOD RATHER THAN CHEWING IT.

dinos had quite sophisticated senses of smell. So standing still is not a sure-fire way of keeping safe – the dinosaur can still smell you. The problem is that, although we can identify it as a meat-eating dinosaur, we don't know enough about its habits to anticipate how it might attack. From here you are on your own – so good luck!

tigers and leopards. Plant-eaters may have been dressed in duller colours or even camouflaged.

A dangerous situation

With all this knowledge you should be able to tell what kind of dinosaur faces you. But then what do you do? A plant-eater will probably just run away, or ignore you. But if it is a meat-eater you could be in great danger – it might attack you. You've probably heard that a meat-eating dinosaur's eyes work on movement, so if its would-be prey stands still, it can't detect it. Don't believe a word of this! Scientists now know that many meat-eating

C ut it up

Of course you'd get a better idea of what kind of animal you had if it lay dead at your feet. Then you could see its jaws and teeth, and count its fingers. If you could look inside it, what you would find would be even more interesting. Cut open the belly of the dinosaur (you wouldn't

TYRANNOSAURUS, A MEAT-EATER, CRUNCHED BONE, RIPPED SINEWS, AND TORE OFF CHUNKS OF MEAT – USING ONLY ITS JAWS.

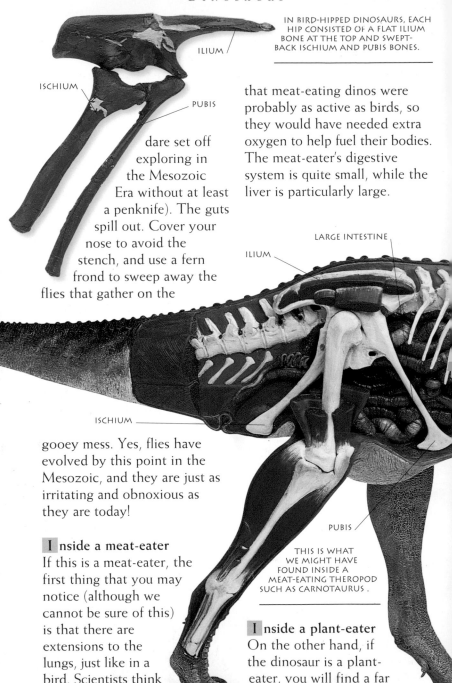

IN BIRD-HIPPED DINOSAURS, EACH HIP CONSISTED OF A FLAT ILIUM BONE AT THE TOP AND SWEPT-BACK ISCHIUM AND PUBIS BONES.

ILIUM

ISCHIUM

PUBIS

that meat-eating dinos were probably as active as birds, so they would have needed extra oxygen to help fuel their bodies. The meat-eater's digestive system is quite small, while the liver is particularly large.

dare set off exploring in the Mesozoic Era without at least a penknife). The guts spill out. Cover your nose to avoid the stench, and use a fern frond to sweep away the flies that gather on the

LARGE INTESTINE

ILIUM

ISCHIUM

gooey mess. Yes, flies have evolved by this point in the Mesozoic, and they are just as irritating and obnoxious as they are today!

PUBIS

THIS IS WHAT WE MIGHT HAVE FOUND INSIDE A MEAT-EATING THEROPOD SUCH AS CARNOTAURUS.

Inside a meat-eater

If this is a meat-eater, the first thing that you may notice (although we cannot be sure of this) is that there are extensions to the lungs, just like in a bird. Scientists think

Inside a plant-eater

On the other hand, if the dinosaur is a plant-eater, you will find a far greater volume of intestine. A plant diet needs a much more complex digestive system than a meat diet does. If you can recognize the heart among all the gore and innards, you will probably find that it is a big one, indicating that this animal, too, had an active lifestyle.

The tell-tale hips

If you are still up for it, keep cutting away the flesh beneath the legs until you

LUNG

HEART

STOMACH   LIVER

find the hip-bones. This could be the proof. In most theropod meat-eaters, the hip-bones are arranged like those of lizards, with the pubis, one of the two lower hip-bones, pointing forwards and the other, the ischium, pointing backwards. An ornithopod plant-eater has hips like those of a bird, with both the pubis and the

ischium swept backwards out of the way. This leaves a big space beneath the hips for the plant-eater's large digestive system.

Out come the scavengers

But now it's time to make a rapid exit. The smells of meat and death have alerted all the scavenging animals in the area, which start to converge on the corpse. The body is torn to bits. Flesh and organs are eaten, and the bones are carried off. The remains rot away into the soil. After some days, there is nothing left but a stain on the ground. Nothing left to fossilize. No wonder we only know of about one-fifth of the dinosaurs that ever existed!

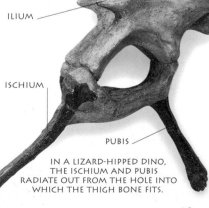

ILIUM

ISCHIUM

PUBIS

IN A LIZARD-HIPPED DINO, THE ISCHIUM AND PUBIS RADIATE OUT FROM THE HOLE INTO WHICH THE THIGH BONE FITS.

HOW FOSSILS FORM

So how on Earth did any dinosaurs ever manage to become fossilized? Let's imagine a *Corythosaurus*, a plant-eater living on the wooded lowlands of western North America 78 million years ago. Our dinosaur has reached a respectable old age – perhaps 50 years, although this is just an educated guess, since scientists can't yet determine the lifespans of individual dinosaurs.

Death of a dinosaur

The *Corythosaurus* is one of several gathered by a lowland stream. The old dinosaur is frail and vulnerable to disease. As it crouches on the bank to take a drink, the great effort of lowering its head to the water

CORYTHOSAURUS HAD A DUCK-LIKE BEAK FOR STRIPPING LEAVES OFF PLANTS AND A DISTINCTIVE CREST ON ITS HEAD. IT TRAVELLED IN LARGE HERDS THROUGH PLAINS, FORESTS, AND SWAMPS.

proves too much for it. Age finally takes its toll – the blood supply to its little brain fails and life withdraws from its weary body. With a final gasp it collapses in a lifeless heap at the water's edge.

Corpse on the move

For days the rain has been falling in the mountains, and now the lowland stream is becoming swollen with mountain flood-water. The muddy torrent sweeps around the body of the *Corythosaurus*, gathers it up, and washes it downstream. Some distance away the current slows, and the heaviest of the flood debris begins to settle. The waters fall back to their normal level, and the corpse is left high and dry in the sun.

Laid to rest

The flesh of the dead dinosaur dries out quickly in the sunshine and hardens. Few scavenging animals would find this appetizing, so the body is left alone. As the corpse continues to dry out, the tendons that link the bones together shrink, pulling the neck backwards and twisting the head over the back. The limbs, too, are contorted into odd positions. Later, in the next flood, the waters swirl around the body again. By now the tendons have rotted, the

LOG ON...
In-depth fact files at
www.bbc.co.uk/dinosaurs/

A DEAD DINOSAUR FALLING INTO A RIVER
COULD SINK AND BE COVERED WITH
SEDIMENT, SUCH AS SAND, SILT, OR
MUD, BEFORE THE BODY
BEGAN TO ROT.

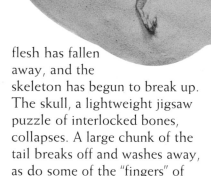

flesh has fallen
away, and the
skeleton has begun to break up.
The skull, a lightweight jigsaw
puzzle of interlocked bones,
collapses. A large chunk of the
tail breaks off and washes away,
as do some of the "fingers" of

the forelimbs.
Luckily, before the
skeleton is destroyed
completely, the receding
flood-water deposits a thick
layer of sediment (mostly
river sand) over the
Corythosaurus. It remains
safely buried for a long,
long, long time.

What you've just read
represents the "taphonomy" of
the dinosaur. To save you from
dashing for the dictionary,
that's the word for the study of
what happens to the body of an
animal after it dies and before
the body becomes fossilized.
The technical term for what
happens next in the fossilizing

WEIRD WORLD
THE EARTH ROTATED FASTER IN
DINOSAUR TIMES. BECAUSE OF THIS,
DAYS WERE SHORTER AND THERE
WERE 380 DAYS IN A YEAR, NOT
365 AS THERE ARE TODAY.

process is actually "diagenesis" – but to keep things simple, we'll just call it…

Turning to stone

Because the flat river plain sea, and marine sediments, including the remains of dead sea creatures, are laid down upon it. As millions of years pass, the weight of all the sediment layers above squeezes the river sand around our

PERHAPS ONLY ONE DINOSAUR IN A MILLION WAS FOSSILIZED

where *Corythosaurus* died floods frequently, the skeleton soon becomes entombed by layer upon layer of sediment. Eventually, the land sinks beneath the *Corythosaurus* skeleton. The sand particles are squashed together, so that the spaces between them become smaller and smaller. Water trickling down through the sediment

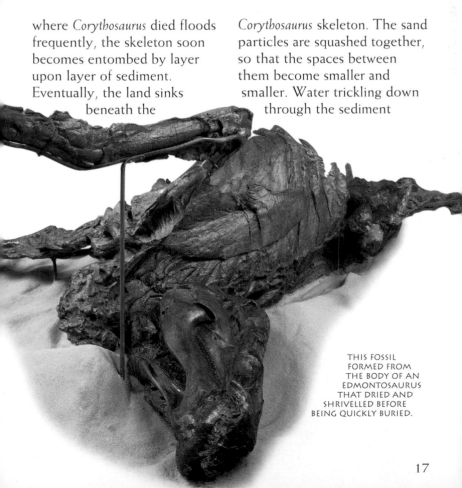

THIS FOSSIL FORMED FROM THE BODY OF AN EDMONTOSAURUS THAT DRIED AND SHRIVELLED BEFORE BEING QUICKLY BURIED.

17

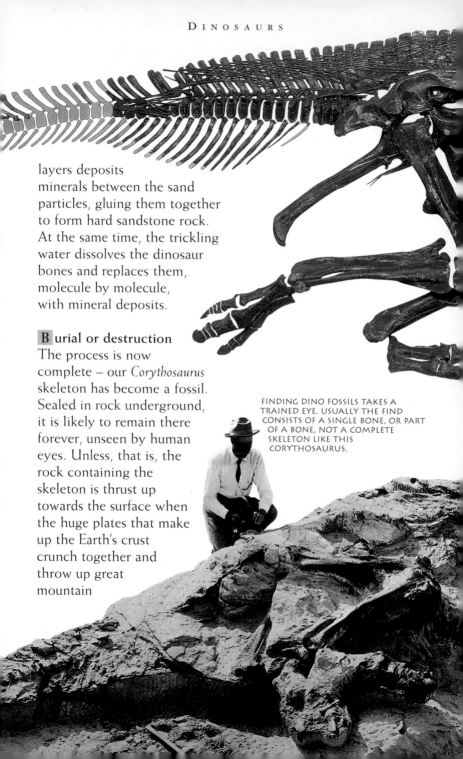

layers deposits
minerals between the sand
particles, gluing them together
to form hard sandstone rock.
At the same time, the trickling
water dissolves the dinosaur
bones and replaces them,
molecule by molecule,
with mineral deposits.

B urial or destruction

The process is now
complete – our *Corythosaurus*
skeleton has become a fossil.
Sealed in rock underground,
it is likely to remain there
forever, unseen by human
eyes. Unless, that is, the
rock containing the
skeleton is thrust up
towards the surface when
the huge plates that make
up the Earth's crust
crunch together and
throw up great
mountain

FINDING DINO FOSSILS TAKES A
TRAINED EYE. USUALLY THE FIND
CONSISTS OF A SINGLE BONE, OR PART
OF A BONE, NOT A COMPLETE
SKELETON LIKE THIS
CORYTHOSAURUS.

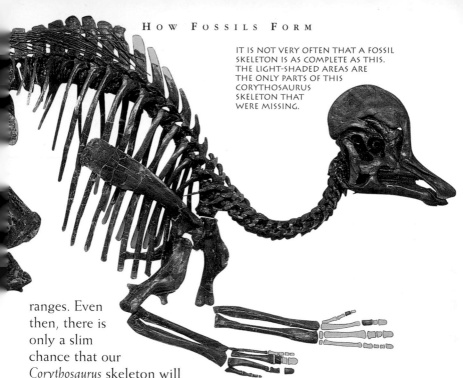

IT IS NOT VERY OFTEN THAT A FOSSIL SKELETON IS AS COMPLETE AS THIS. THE LIGHT-SHADED AREAS ARE THE ONLY PARTS OF THIS CORYTHOSAURUS SKELETON THAT WERE MISSING.

ranges. Even then, there is only a slim chance that our *Corythosaurus* skeleton will ever be found. Rain, wind, and frost soon begin to wear down the mountains, breaking up the mountain rocks and any fossils they contain, and grinding them into tiny fragments that are washed away.

Discovery

Sadly, that will be the fate of our *Corythosaurus* skeleton. The only hope is that someone passes by at just the right time – as a fossil bone is starting to emerge from the rock – and is sharp-eyed enough to realize what it is. If that person alerts a museum about the discovery, the fossil stands a good chance of being excavated and preserved. So you can see how heavily the odds are stacked against any dinosaur getting fossilized, and any fossils being discovered. We should consider ourselves lucky to have found any at all!

WEIRD WORLD

THERE ARE ABOUT 1,200 DINOSAUR SPECIMENS IN MUSEUMS. THIS SOUNDS LIKE A LOT UNTIL YOU CONSIDER THAT THERE MAY HAVE BEEN 1,500 DIFERENT DINOSAURS, EACH OF WHICH COULD HAVE LIVED FOR 2–10 MILLION YEARS…

THE DINOSAUR REVEALED

Imagine that you have discovered a dinosaur skeleton – a *Corythosaurus* or a *Tyrannosaurus* – in sandstone rock. You will need to dig it out, but excavation takes a long time. The bones must be removed without breaking them and then transported to a place where they can be studied – a museum or a laboratory in a university.

Protecting the bones

Although the bones have been fossilized, they are still very brittle. They must be protected while they are dug out and removed. Plaster-soaked sacking is best for this. Once you have chiselled away the over-lying rock, you must cover the exposed surface of the fossil in this material. Then you and your team – it's too big a job to tackle on your own – remove each bone or part of the skeleton completely from the rock, turn it over, and encase the rest of it in plaster.

AFTER DIGGING A TRENCH AROUND A BONE, PALAEONTOLOGISTS COAT IT IN SACKING AND RUNNY PLASTER

At every stage you photograph what you are doing to keep a record of where it all came from.

Back at the laboratory, you must take off the plaster to allow skilled technicians (called preparators) to remove any remaining rock and to treat the

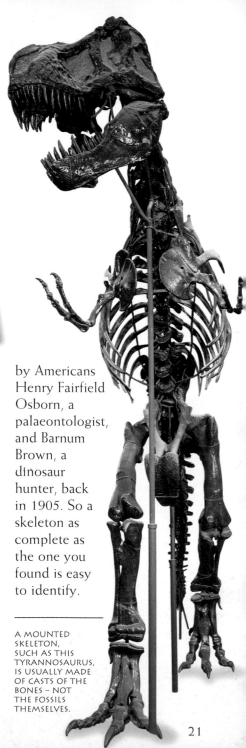

fossil so that it does not decay. Now you can devote yourself to rebuilding the dinosaur. This will show you what the animal was like when it was alive.

Identification

But what type of dinosaur is it? The experts are quick to tell you that your skeleton is of a *Tyrannosaurus*. Although the ribs, the arms, most of one leg, and pieces of the skull have disappeared, your skeleton is still relatively complete. About 80 per cent of the bones are present – more than we get with most dinosaur skeletons. More than 20 *Tyrannosaurus* skeletons have been found since the first one was unearthed and named by Americans Henry Fairfield Osborn, a palaeontologist, and Barnum Brown, a dinosaur hunter, back in 1905. So a skeleton as complete as the one you found is easy to identify.

A MOUNTED SKELETON, SUCH AS THIS TYRANNOSAURUS, IS USUALLY MADE OF CASTS OF THE BONES – NOT THE FOSSILS THEMSELVES.

21

THIS TYRANNOSAURUS LEG SKELETON WILL SHOW THE MARKS WHERE THE MUSCLES WERE ONCE ATTACHED.

Dino display

If you want to put your *Tyrannosaurus* on public display in a museum, you must first decide whether to build up the skeleton with the actual fossils or with casts of them.

Nowadays, it is so easy to make good casts of fossil bones from lightweight materials, such as glass fibre, that this is what is usually done. It makes the display easier to build and keeps the original fossils safe for scientific study. But what about any missing parts of the skeleton? Easy – you speak to the owners of the other 20 or so *Tyrannosaurus* skeletons and arrange to make casts of the bones missing from your own *Tyrannosaurus* skeleton.

Reconstructing and restoring

At last you have your mounted skeleton for display to the public. This is what is known as a reconstruction. Now you want to build up a picture of what the animal was like when it was alive. A painting, sculpture, or video presentation that shows what the animal was like in life is known as a restoration. The two terms are often confused.

A COMPLETE DINOSAUR SKULL, SUCH AS THIS ONE FROM TYRANNOSAURUS, IS A VERY RARE FIND. MOST SKULLS FELL APART BEFORE THEY GOT A CHANCE TO FOSSILIZE.

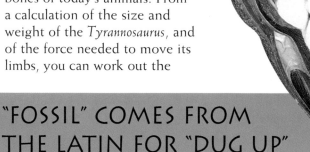

The muscles

The first step in creating our restoration is to take a close look at the individual bones. There are marks on them that show where the muscles were attached. You can compare these with the marks on the bones of today's animals. From a calculation of the size and weight of the *Tyrannosaurus*, and of the force needed to move its limbs, you can work out the

"FOSSIL" COMES FROM THE LATIN FOR "DUG UP"

size of the muscles it needed. Once you have fleshed out the entire skeleton, you will have a good idea of the shape of the living animal.

Be careful with the skull. Like most dinosaur skulls, that of *Tyrannosaurus* consists of struts of bone, and so is full of holes. In 1920, one of the most famous dinosaur artists of all time, the American Charles R. Knight, painted a *Tyrannosaurus* with its eye in the wrong skull hole. Few people noticed the mistake. The painting was later

used as the inspiration for the *Tyrannosaurus* that appeared in the hugely successful 1933 film *King Kong*. So Knight's error went down in movie history.

The skin

All animals are covered with skin. The dinosaurs were, too.

23

Unfortunately, skin is too soft to be easily preserved and so it is rare to find it as a fossil. But now and again there is a lucky occurrence where a dinosaur has rolled in mud, leaving the impression of its skin behind. The impression was preserved when the mud eventually turned to rock (remember the word diagenesis?), leaving us a fossil of the dinosaur's skin texture. There is a skin impression from South America of a big meat-eating dinosaur – not *Tyrannosaurus*, but a big meat-eater of a similar size. This is the closest that we are likely to get, and so we can use this skin impression to give us an idea of the surface texture of our animal.

The colour

Finally, we must determine the colour of our dinosaur. Colour is certainly never preserved – an animal's colour hardly ever outlives the animal itself. It is one of the first things to change after the animal dies.

What we can do is look at the colour schemes worn by

THIS IMPRESSION OF CORYTHOSAURUS SKIN SHOWS THAT THE ANIMAL WAS COVERED IN SMALL, BUMPY SCALES.

modern animals. By examining an animal's lifestyle and the environment in which it lives, we can determine whether it uses its colours for camouflage, or whether it uses them to signal to other animals. We can then apply this knowledge to dinosaurs. It is possible that dinosaurs with similar lifestyles to modern animals and living in similar environments also had the same colour schemes.

A *Tyrannosaurus* colour scheme

A meat-eating dinosaur may have been brightly coloured, with stripes or spots, because modern hunting cats have these colour schemes. But big animals tend to be duller in colour than small animals – compare an elephant with a zebra. Taking this into consideration, we can guess that a big meat-eating dinosaur like *Tyrannosaurus* may have had a dull colouring consisting of stripes or spots. We may be wrong, but we've given it our best shot. It's the best we can do with the evidence available!

SCIENTISTS HAVE LITTLE EVIDENCE ABOUT DINOSAUR COLOURS. LOOK AT THESE COLOUR SCHEMES FOR THE MEAT-EATER VELOCIRAPTOR . FOR ALL WE KNOW, ANY ONE OF THEM COULD BE CORRECT.

DINOS GALORE!

Palaeontologists have been discovering, excavating, reconstructing, and restoring dinosaurs for about 150 years, so today we have a good idea of the range of dinosaurs that existed. We can divide the dinosaurs into two major groups, according to the arrangement of their hip-bones. One group had lizard-like hips, while the other group had hips that resembled those of a bird.

Lizard-hipped dinos

All meat-eating dinosaurs had lizard-like hips. The meat-eaters are known as theropods, a name that means "beast-footed". The 19th-century scientist who first used this name for

BARYONYX , A FISH-EATING THEROPOD, HAD A HEAD LIKE A CROCODILE. IT WAS ABOUT 10.5 M (34 FT) LONG AND 3 M (10 FT) TALL.

meat-eating dinosaurs assumed that they were predators because they had big, sharp, hooked claws on their toes. He noticed that most plant-eaters had only blunt hooves or toenails.

Theropod dinosaurs had strong hind legs

LOG ON...
www.dinofun.com for
dino games, clipart, and links

and long jaws bearing sharp teeth. But there was incredible variation among the dinosaurs of the theropod group.

Theropod parade

Some theropods were big and powerful, like *Tyrannosaurus*. Others were small and graceful, like the chicken-sized *Compsognathus*. In between was a vast range of dinosaurs, hunting all types of animal and using a range of strategies. There were fast little hunters, commonly called "raptors", that killed with a sickle-shaped claw on the hind foot. The raptors included the goose-sized *Bambiraptor*, the wolf-sized *Velociraptor*, the tiger-sized *Deinonychus*, and the huge *Utahraptor*. There were fast sprinters, such as *Ornithomimus* and *Gallimimus*, that resembled ostriches. There was also a group of fish-hunting dinosaurs with crocodile-like jaws and a thumb claw for hooking fish out of the water. These included *Baryonyx* and *Suchomimus*. The earliest known dinosaurs, *Herrerasaurus* and *Eoraptor*, may have been theropods, or they may have been so primitive that they formed a different group entirely.

WITH ITS NECK HELD UP HIGH, THE OSTRICH-LIKE *GALLIMIMUS* COULD SWIVEL ITS HEAD AND SEE IN ALL DIRECTIONS.

The sauropods

The lizard-hipped dinosaurs also included huge, long-necked

DIPLODOCUS WAS A SAUROPOD WITH A SMALL HEAD, WEAK JAWS, AND PENCIL-LIKE TEETH, WHICH IT USED TO RIP LEAVES OFF FERNS AND TREES.

dinos called sauropods, which means "lizard-footed".

The sauropods' enormous gut, which they needed to digest the vast quantities of plant food they ate, forced them to be four-footed. The gut had to be carried well forward of the lizard-like hips and out of the way of both forward-pointing

scientists think that the prosauropods were exclusively plant-eaters, but that they sometimes walked on their hind legs, as the theropods did, and sometimes on all fours, just like the sauropods.

BABY DIPLODOCUS WERE 2 M (6.5 FT) LONG ON HATCHING

pubis bones. This made it difficult for the sauropods to balance on their hind legs, so they went about on all fours.

Prototype sauropods
The prosauropods were an earlier group of lizard-hipped dinos that were once thought to eat both meat and

plants, thus forming a link between the theropods and the sauropods. Today,

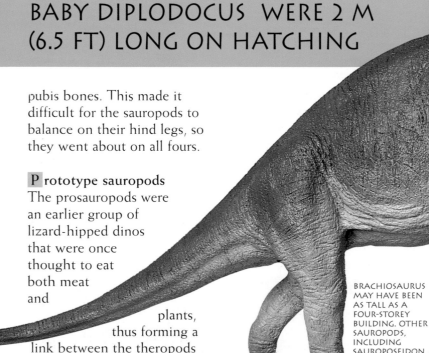

BRACHIOSAURUS MAY HAVE BEEN AS TALL AS A FOUR-STOREY BUILDING. OTHER SAUROPODS, INCLUDING SAUROPOSEIDON, WERE BIGGER STILL.

F amiliar faces

The most familiar sauropods were the long, low ones such as *Diplodocus* and *Seismosaurus*, and the tall, high-shouldered types like *Brachiosaurus* and *Sauroposeidon*. These were the most important plant-eaters in Jurassic times, but they began to die away during the Cretaceous.

One group of sauropods, the titanosaurs, survived until the very end of the dinosaur period, being particularly widespread in South America. The titanosaurs, such as *Saltasaurus*, had backs that were covered in bony armour. This was possibly to help stiffen and strengthen the animal's backbone, rather than as a defensive measure – there were few predators about that would dare to threaten a fully grown sauropod.

B ird-hipped dinos

Unlike sauropods, the bird-hipped dinosaurs could carry their plant-digesting gut beneath their hips, close to their centre of gravity. This allowed some of them, known as ornithopods, to walk on their hind legs. Ornithopod means "bird-footed".

The largest ornithopods – animals such as *Iguanodon* and the duck-billed dinosaurs *Hadrosaurus* and *Corythosaurus* – probably spent most of their lives on all fours, because of the sheer weight of their bodies. In fact, modern studies show that duck-bills' front feet were paw-like and built for taking weight. However, their youngsters were probably sprightly two-footed animals.

The smaller ornithopods, such as *Hypsilophodon*, were built for two-footed speed and were the

WEIRD WORLD
THE LARGEST OF THE SAUROPOD DINOSAURS COULD HAVE WEIGHED UP TO 100 TONNES. EXPERTS THINK THAT THE HEART ALONE MIGHT HAVE WEIGHED NEARLY 1 TONNE!

dinosaur equivalent of gazelles. The ornithopods' heyday came during the Cretaceous Period, when they took over from the sauropods as the main group of plant-eating dinosaurs.

However, many stegosaurs, including *Kentrosaurus*, only had narrow plates and spikes. These were probably used more for defence or display than for temperature control.

THERE WERE MANY MORE PLANT-EATERS THAN MEAT-EATERS

The stegosaurs

Another group of bird-hipped dinos was the stegosaurs. Also known as "plated dinosaurs", these were among the most flamboyant of the plant-eaters, with a double row of plates or spikes running along the back. These may have been used as armour or, if they were covered in skin, to control body temperature. Held towards the sun in the morning, the plates

The stegosaurs were mostly four-footed animals. Their cumbersome plates would have made it difficult for them to be otherwise. However, some of them, such as *Stegosaurus* itself, had very powerful muscles in the hip region. This would have allowed them to stand on their hind legs for short periods

may have absorbed heat and warmed the animal's blood. Held into the wind at midday, they would have given off heat and cooled the blood.

AN ORNITHOPOD, SUCH AS HYPSILOPHODON, CAN BE DISTINGUISHED FROM A MEAT-EATING THEROPOD BY ITS FATTER BODY.

so they could munch away on low-growing branches.

The ankylosaurs

The truly armoured dinosaurs were the ankylosaurs. These bird-hipped dinos had bone embedded in the thick, leathery skin of the head, the neck, the body, and the tail. Some of these tough cookies were so heavily defended that even the eyelids were armoured, slamming shut like the steel shutters of a battleship when danger approached.

Spikes, clubs, and blades

There were two main groups of ankylosaurs. The first, including *Edmontonia*, had spikes and blades along the sides of the body and tail. These spikes were bigger in the shoulder and neck region, and were used to charge an enemy.

The second group is typified by *Ankylosaurus*, which had no spikes along its sides but instead had a bony club on the end of its tail. The tail bones were fused, making the tail stiff and strong, like the shaft of a medieval mace. This enabled the bony club to be swung with great force to deliver a mighty whack to the flanks and legs of an attacking theropod. Although known from early Jurassic times, it was in the Cretaceous Period that the ankylosaurs really became important, taking the place of the stegosaurs that had by then begun to die away.

The ceratopsians

The end of the Cretaceous saw the

from two-footed dinosaurs. One of the earliest examples was *Psittacosaurus*, which had a big beak and a ridge around the back of the skull, giving it a parrot-like appearance. By the late Cretaceous Period, the ceratopsians' skull ridge had extended to form an armoured shield or "frill" that protected the neck and shoulders. The later ceratopsians were divided into two groups – those, such as *Styracosaurus*, that had a large nose horn and a short frill, and those, such as

development of another group of bird-hipped dinosaurs, called ceratopsians. The ceratopsians evolved

Triceratops, that had large brow horns as well as a nose horn and a long frill. The different horn arrangements helped to distinguish one species from another as herds mixed on the North American plains.

The bone-heads

Closely related to ceratopsians were the pachycephalosaurs, which included *Stegoceras* and *Pachycephalosaurus*. What made

THE EARLIEST CERATOPSIANS, SUCH AS THE PARROT-LIKE PSITTACOSAURUS, HAD VERY LITTLE ARMOUR ON THEIR HEADS.

these two-footed plant-eaters different was the solid mass of bone on the top of the head. This "bone dome" was possibly used as a battering ram when dealing with enemies or with rivals within the herd.

Did this head-banging give them splitting headaches? We'll never know for sure, but probably not, because the bones of their skulls could be up to 23 cm (9 in) thick.

EUOPLOCEPHALUS AND OTHER LARGE ANKYLOSAURS WERE SO HEAVILY ARMOURED THAT THEY WERE LIKE WALKING TANKS.

LIFESTYLE CLUES

N ow you have the mounted reconstruction of the dinosaur, and you have the restoration that shows what it looked like in life. But that is only part of the story. You need other evidence to tell you how your dinosaur lived. To find this, you must go back to the excavation site. There are plenty of clues in the sandstone rocks where you found your skeleton.

D etective work

A careful examination of the sandstone should show up bits of plant material and pollen grains. These will build up a picture of the plant life of the area. Sifting the sands may throw up tiny bones of small animals such as lizards or shrew-like mammals, or the wings of insects. These will give us an idea of what other animals existed alongside your dinosaur. Bones of freshwater fish and shells of water snails will help to prove that this was a river environment, and not a seashore one.

F ootprints in the sands of time

The best evidence comes from traces left by the dinosaurs themselves. The study of fossil footprints has a

IGUANODON HAD THREE SHORT TOES ON EACH FOOT. IT WOULD HAVE LEFT CLOVER-SHAPED FOOTPRINTS ON MUD OR DAMP SAND.

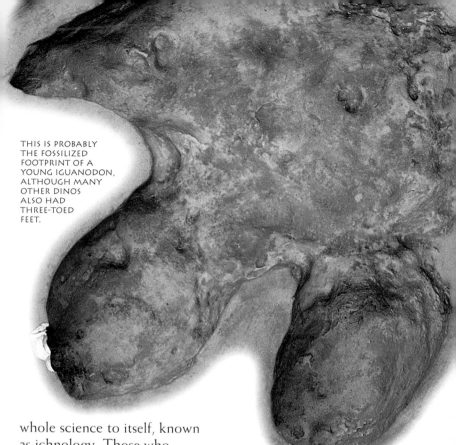

THIS IS PROBABLY THE FOSSILIZED FOOTPRINT OF A YOUNG IGUANODON, ALTHOUGH MANY OTHER DINOS ALSO HAD THREE-TOED FEET.

whole science to itself, known as ichnology. Those who study fossil footprints (ichnologists) claim that their science reveals more about the living dinosaur than any number of bones can. You can see their point. In its lifetime a single animal can leave thousands of footprints behind, but only one skeleton. From the footprints, we can tell if an animal has been walking or running. If running, we can estimate the speed. We can tell if it had been travelling along a

A PALAEONTOLOGIST EXAMINES FOSSILIZED DINOSAUR FOOTPRINTS. THE SPEED OF THE ANIMAL CAN BE CALCULATED FROM THE DISTANCE BETWEEN ITS FOOTPRINTS.

river bank, crossing a river, or gathering around a water hole. We can tell if it moved about singly, in a pair, in a family group, or as part of a herd. What we cannot tell, however, is exactly which dinosaur made which set of footprints. We can have a good guess, but there will always be an uncertainty. That is why ichnologists give fossil footprints their own scientific names. *Brontopodus* may be the footprints of a sauropod like *Apatosaurus*, but we are not sure.

Tetrapodosauropus may be the footprints of an armoured dinosaur like *Nodosaurus*, but we cannot be 100 per cent certain.

Dinosaur eggs

How do you like your eggs – fried, scrambled, or boiled? Palaeontologists prefer theirs to be fossilized! Dinosaur eggs, although rare, give us another

MAIASAURA MEANS "GOOD MOTHER LIZARD". SCIENTISTS THINK THAT FEMALE MAIASAURA BROUGHT FOOD TO THEIR NEWLY HATCHED BABIES.

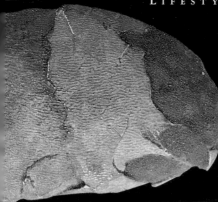

Oviraptor is innocent!
The first dinosaur eggs were found in the Gobi Desert, Mongolia, in the 1920s by an expedition from the American Museum of Natural History. Among fossilized herds of the horned dinosaur *Protoceratops*, they found nests of eggs. During the late Cretaceous, the eggs had been laid in a circle in a hole scooped in sand. One even had the skeleton of a small theropod crouched over it. The theropod was named *Oviraptor*, or "egg thief", as it seemed to have died in the act of raiding a

glimpse into dinosaur life. Once again, there is a great deal of difficulty in matching eggs to particular dinosaurs. Sometimes we are lucky and find whole nesting sites with nests, eggs, babies, and adults, all fossilized together.

Perhaps the best-known nesting site is in Montana, USA. It is the nesting site of the duck-billed *Maiasaura*. The nests, built of mud and twigs and about 2 m (6.5 ft) across, are spaced at regular distances from each other. In or by the nests are egg shells, baby dinosaurs, partly grown dinosaurs, and adults. Experts believe that this represents an annual nesting site, to which the *Maiasaura* herd migrated every year. More often, the evidence is vague or misleading.

Protoceratops nest. Seventy years later, another such nest was found in Mongolia. This nest contained the

THIS IS THE SKULL OF PROTOCERATOPS, A FOUR-LEGGED PLANT-EATER WITH A LARGE BONY NECK FRILL FOR PROTECTION AND A SHARP BEAK FOR SNIPPING UP VEGETATION.

THIS SKELETON OF AN OVIRAPTOR SITTING
ON THE GOBI DESERT EGGS SHOWS
THAT THESE EGGS WERE NOT FROM
PROTOCERATOPS AFTER ALL.

ARM

CLAWS

same eggs, but
this time an
Oviraptor was
sitting upon
them, brooding
like a modern
bird. The eggs were
found to have *Oviraptor*
embryos inside them.
So the eggs found in the
1920s were *Oviraptor* eggs
all the time!

EGGS

FOOT

In a similar story, some large
eggs found in southern France
were, for a long time, attributed
to the sauropod *Hypselosaurus*.
But recently it has been
suggested that they were
actually laid by a big
cassowary-like bird
that lived

in France at about the same
time as *Hypselosaurus*. So you
see, some of what we know
today about dinosaurs may
be overturned by what we
discover in the future.

Dinosaur droppings
Coprolite. There is an
impressive name. It
actually means "dung
stone". A coprolite
is the fossil of an
animal's droppings!
Coprolites may
sound like repulsive
remains to you, but
palaeontologists love
them, and some devote
themselves entirely to studying
this prehistoric poo. The most
common coprolites come from
aquatic animals such as fish, but

OVIRAPTOR HAD A
STRANGE FACE, WITH A
SHORT BEAK THAT SEEMED
TO SUGGEST IT WAS AN
EGG-EATER. NOW WE ARE
NOT SO SURE.

LOG ON...
See Zoom Dinosaurs at www.enchantedlearning.com

several dinosaur coprolites have been found. Food fragments in a coprolite can tell us about the diet of its "owner", and the coprolite's shape can reveal something about the layout of the animal's digestive system.

There is one coprolite that is thought to be *Tyrannosaurus* dung, but as with footprints and eggs, it is impossible to be sure. It is 20 cm (8 in) long and full of pieces of duck-billed dinosaur bones – just what we'd expect from guessing about *Tyrannosaurus'* hunting habits.

S tomach stones

Another guide to the diet of a dinosaur is the presence of stomach

stones, or gastroliths, in the skeleton. The sauropods did not have the type of teeth that could be used for chewing. Instead, they raked leaves and twigs from branches and swallowed them whole. To help them process their food,

they also swallowed stones. These gathered in an area of the stomach called the gizzard and helped grind up the food as it passed through. Today, plant-eating birds such as pigeons swallow grit for the same purpose – they cannot chew with their beaks.

Gastroliths may be found with the fossilized skeletons of sauropods. They may also appear as neat piles where the animals vomited them up when they became too smooth to be of any use. New, rougher stones were then swallowed to keep the grinding process going.

COPROLITES MAY JUST LOOK LIKE STONES TO US, BUT TO PALAEONTOLOGISTS THEY'RE TREASURE TROVES OF DINO INFORMATION.

> ### WEIRD WORLD
> A DINOSAUR TRACKSITE IN TEXAS, USA, COVERS AN AREA OF 100,000 SQ KM (38,600 SQ MILES). IT IS ONLY SEEN ON THE SURFACE IN A FEW PLACES – THE REST IS BURIED IN THE ROCKS.

OTHER LIFE AT THE TIME

B y this stage, you may be thinking that dinosaurs were practically the only creatures on Earth during the Mesozoic Era. Far from it – there was a whole host of other animals around at the time. As with the dinosaurs, it's through fossils that we know of their existence.

AMMONITES WERE TENTACLED SEA CREATURES WITH SPIRAL-SHAPED SHELLS. FOSSILIZED AMMONITES ARE COMMON IN MARINE ROCKS FROM DINOSAUR TIMES.

Water beasts

We have already seen how difficult it is for a land animal such as a dinosaur to become fossilized. The best dinosaur fossils come from animals that lived near water, because their dead bodies could become buried in sediment and involved in the rock-forming processes. How much easier, then, must it be for an animal that actually lived in the water to become fossilized. If you go out and look for fossils in a well-known fossil site, you'll rarely find the fossil of a dinosaur or any other large animal. What you will find are the fossils of shellfish and other animals that lived in the sea. It's not surprising, really. Shellfish live on the sea bed, where sediments

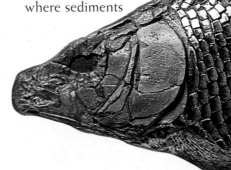

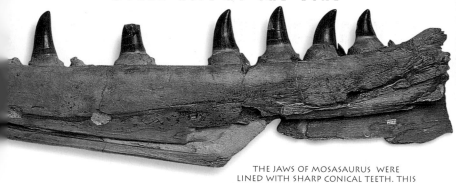

THE JAWS OF MOSASAURUS WERE LINED WITH SHARP CONICAL TEETH. THIS REPTILE SWAM IN SHALLOW COASTAL WATERS AND WAS UP TO 10 M (33 FT) LONG.

are continually accumulating, so their remains naturally get buried under sand, mud, or silt.

The first sea monster

The Mesozoic was truly the Age of Reptiles. Not only were dinosaurs masters of the land, but reptiles also dominated the seas and commanded the skies. The Mesozoic sea reptiles were known to scientists long before the dinosaurs were. In 1770, a fossilized jaw was unearthed in a chalk mine near Maastricht in the Netherlands. It fell into the hands of the invading French army and eventually ended up in Paris, where it was studied by Baron Georges Cuvier, the leading biologist of the day.

At that time, scientists were beginning to understand that different animals had lived on the Earth at different times, and that many of the animals that lived in the past were now extinct. Cuvier realized that the fossil skull was from a type of enormous swimming lizard, which became known as *Mosasaurus*. This was one of a

WE KNOW THAT THE FISH LEPIDOTES LIVED DURING DINOSAUR TIMES, BECAUSE ITS SCALES HAVE BEEN FOUND IN THE STOMACH OF BARYONYX .

41

large family of reptiles, called the mosaurs, which swam by thrashing their tails to and fro. The other big reptiles of the Mesozoic were ichthyosaurs and plesiosaurs. On the coast of Dorset, in southern

THE PLESIOSAUR CRYPTOCLIDUS HAD A SNAKE-LIKE NECK AND INTERLOCKING SPIKED TEETH THAT CLAMPED TIGHT AROUND FISH AND OTHER SEA CREATURES.

England, skeletons of these marine reptiles were being dug up and studied in the early 19th century.

Fishy lizards

The ichthyosaurs, or fish lizards, were originally regarded as a type of crocodile.

It is easy to see why, with their long jaws and sharp teeth – the signs of a meat-eating reptile. But when more and more skeletons were discovered, it became clear that they were a totally different kind of animal. Although they were reptiles, they were so well-adapted to their watery way of life that they developed body shapes

WEIRD WORLD

WHEN A BASKING SHARK DIES, ITS HUGE JAWS FALL OFF. THE TINY-HEADED CARCASS LOOKS LIKE A ROTTING PLESIOSAUR. THIS EXPLAINS REPORTS OF DEAD PLESIOSAURS BEING FOUND ON MODERN BEACHES.

ICHTHYOSAURUS SWAM WITH SIDEWAYS MOVEMENTS OF ITS TAIL. LIKE OTHER MARINE REPTILES, IT HAD TO SURFACE TO FILL ITS LUNGS WITH AIR.

were replaced by the mosasaurs.

just like those of fish or dolphins – a streamlined body, paddles for limbs, a fin on the tail and one on the back. The fins were not originally obvious, but fossil ichthyosaurs discovered near Holzmaden, in Germany, were so detailed that even these soft body parts were preserved. The ichthyosaurs evolved in the Triassic, when some grew as big as whales. They flourished in the Jurassic and died out before the end of the Cretaceous, when they

Long necks and short necks

There were two types of plesiosaur. The long-necked types which, according to one 19th-century scientist, resembled snakes threaded through turtles, and the short-necked types, which had big heads and long jaws. Again, these are much more common as fossils than land-living animals such as dinosaurs. They evolved in the Triassic and continued until the end of the Cretaceous Period.

Flying reptiles

As well as reptiles powering through the oceans, there were also reptiles flapping, soaring, and swooping through the sky. The pterosaurs were a group of reptiles that, although distantly related, were not themselves dinosaurs. Their wings were thin flaps of skin supported by elongated fourth fingers. Pterosaurs probably ate fish and insects, and may have been covered in fur, like bats are today. We have a fair number of pterosaur

fossils, because many of them lived in coastal areas and fell into the sea when they died.

For the first part of the Age of Reptiles, these animals were the undisputed rulers of the skies, with flying insects their only competitors. But in the Jurassic Period, birds evolved

DIMORPHODON PROBABLY SNATCHED FISH IN ITS PUFFIN-LIKE BEAK AS IT SKIMMED LOW OVER THE SEA. THE LONG TAIL GAVE STABILITY IN THE AIR.

from dinosaur ancestors, and by Cretaceous times these feathery newcomers shared the skies with the pterosaurs.

The first pterosaurs, the rhamphorhynchoids, had long tails and narrow wings, and included the big-beaked *Dimorphodon*. Later pterosaurs, called pterodactyloids, had short tails and broader, more controllable wings. The pterodactyloids produced the biggest flying creatures

PTERODACTYLUS HAD A WINGSPAN OF ABOUT 50 CM (20 IN). LIKE OTHER PTERODACTYLOIDS, IT HAD A SHORT TAIL AND LONG WRIST-BONES.

Mesozoic Era, but the most important group of vertebrates were the little furry things that scampered around the feet of

PTEROSAURS HAD LIGHTWEIGHT HOLLOW BONES FILLED WITH AIR

that ever lived – some the size of small aeroplanes – during the Cretaceous Period.

Lesser lights

We have looked at the main groups of reptiles that shared the world with the dinosaurs. A vast array of other animals lived at the time, too. The lizards and snakes evolved in the

the reptilian giants…the mammals. The mammals evolved in the late Triassic Period, at about the same time as the dinosaurs. Throughout the Age of Reptiles they were small, insignificant, shrew-like animals. It was not until the dinosaurs died out that the mammals came into their own. But that is another story.

DINOSAUR HOMES

You've seen how palaeontologists put together the pieces of the dinosaur jigsaw to give us a picture of life in Mesozoic times. We know what dinosaurs looked like, what they ate, how they walked, and what their eggs were like. But the picture is incomplete, as we are less certain about which dinosaurs lived in which habitat.

Where dinosaurs lived

Scientists reckon that dinosaurs colonized all the major habitats of the Mesozoic world. It's difficult to be more precise than that because many habitats were not suited to fossil formation. What do we know, for example, about dinosaurs that lived on mountain tops, where the landscape was constantly being eroded? Practically nothing. What do we know of dinosaurs that lived on windswept rocky outcrops, where no sediments could be laid down? Zilch! What do we know of dinosaurs

LIKE BARYONYX, SUCHOMIMUS WAS A FISH-EATER THAT LIVED BESIDE RIVERS AND LAKES.

that lived in forests well away from rivers, where the soil was continually renewing itself with the growth and decay of plants? Not much more. On rare occasions, we find a dinosaur that was fossilized under ideal circumstances, and from which we can learn a lot.

By the river

Take *Baryonyx*, for example. Nothing like it had ever been found before its discovery in 1983 in a clay pit in Surrey, south-eastern England. It was found in river sediments by an amateur fossil collector. It was about half complete, but the bones that were present were enough to tell experts what the whole skeleton would have been like. *Baryonyx* had long jaws with many sharp teeth, just like a fish-eating crocodile. It also had a big claw on its thumb that resembled the hook on a fishing rod. What's more, its stomach was full of fish bones and fish scales, so it was clear what it ate. The Cretaceous sediments in which

THESE ENTWINED SKELETONS SHOW HOW
A PROTOCERATOPS AND A VELOCIRAPTOR
FOUGHT EACH OTHER TO THE DEATH
MORE THAN 70 MILLION YEARS AGO.

with its thumb claws – just like a modern grizzly bear.

Close relative

Baryonyx was so unusual-looking that when an almost identical animal, *Suchomimus*, was found in North Africa in 1997, scientists had absolutely no doubt that it had lived in the same kind of habitat and had the same lifestyle as *Baryonyx*. But *Suchomimus* was bigger and had a low fin down the length of its back. It was still a closely related animal that waded in rivers to hunt fish.

it was found were laid down on a boggy plain populated by ornithopod dinosaurs such as *Iguanodon* and *Hypsilophodon*. So here we have an instant picture of *Baryonyx*. It was a fish-eating theropod wading in shallow rivers and hooking out fish

WEIRD WORLD

ADULT HUMANS HAVE JUST 32 TEETH, BUT A HADROSAUR HAD UP TO 2,000! LIKE OTHER DINOSAURS, A HADROSAUR COULD REPLACE WORN AND DAMAGED TEETH THROUGHOUT ITS ENTIRE LIFE.

VELOCIRAPTORS MAY HAVE HUNTED IN
PACKS SO THAT THEY COULD TACKLE LARGE
PREY. THEY PROBABLY ENCIRCLED VICTIMS
BEFORE POUNCING, SLASHING AWAY WITH
SICKLE-SHAPED CLAWS ON THEIR REAR FEET.

LOG ON...
Classic dino pictures at
www.search4dinosaurs.com

Secrets of the sands

Another snapshot of dinosaur life was developed in 1972. An expedition in the Gobi Desert in Mongolia uncovered the complete skeletons of a horned *Protoceratops* and a meat-eating *Velociraptor* wrapped around one another. Tickle your cat on its tummy. What does it do? It grabs your hand and kicks away with its hind claws. That's exactly what happened here. The *Velociraptor* had seized the head-shield of the *Protoceratops* and was slashing away at it with the killing claws of its feet. The *Protoceratops* had responded by seizing the attacker by the arm with its sharp beak.

The fierce struggle was fatal for both dinosaurs. A sandstorm then buried the pair, and they were preserved until the present day.

Desert dwellers

This gruesome scene tell us that early horned dinosaurs such as *Protoceratops* were prime targets for the predators of the time. But they certainly didn't give in without a fight! We also know, from the numbers of remains buried in sandstorm deposits, that *Protoceratops* was one of the most common animals around, dotting the

GIGANOTOSAURUS WAS UP TO 12.5 M
(41 FT) LONG AND 8 TONNES IN WEIGHT.
WE KNOW LITTLE OF ITS LIFESTYLE.

landscape like sheep feeding on the sparse desert vegetation. Other fossil finds imply that *Velociraptor* may have lived and hunted in packs. If we

imagine a *Velociraptor* pack prowling the desert on the lookout for a lone *Protoceratops* that has wandered away from the herd, then we are probably not far from the truth.

Forest hunter

Usually it's more difficult to say for certain where a dinosaur lived. We can look at the partial skeleton of *Giganotosaurus*, found in South America, and deduce that it must have been one of the biggest meat-eating dinosaurs. We can conjure up a vision of it rampaging through coniferous forests during the Cretaceous Period. We can also imagine it preying on the biggest plant-eaters that ever lived – such as the sauropod *Argentinosaurus*, which lived in South America at the same time. We really do not have too much evidence for this scenario, however.

Plains runner

Then there are the skeletons of the "ostrich-mimic" dinosaurs, such as *Gallimimus* These lightly built Cretaceous theropods are known as the ostrich mimics because of their rounded

OSTRICHES RUN FOR LONG DISTANCES OVER DRY PLAINS, TRAVELLING FROM ONE FEEDING GROUND TO ANOTHER.

bodies and their long necks and legs. (But this comparison conveniently ignores *Gallimimus*'s long tail.) Recent studies suggest that the resemblance between ostriches and ostrich-mimic dinosaurs is superficial, but the idea won't go away. We see photographs of ostriches sprinting across the open plains of Africa, and it's easy to imagine herds of *Gallimimus* doing the same. Perhaps they did. But, as is often the case, hard evidence is lacking.

GALLIMIMUS MAY HAVE RUN AT UP TO 80 KMH (50 MPH) – FASTER THAN A RACEHORSE.

TRIASSIC TREK

Let us take a walk in the late Triassic Period (about 215 million years ago), after the first dinosaurs had evolved. We know enough from the palaeontology and geology of the time to be able to imagine this. We had better start our walk by the sea. It is the only place that we would find comfortable, or even remotely habitable.

A different world

The late Triassic world is very different from the one we know. If we wanted to go from, say, Los Angeles, USA, to Sydney, Australia, in the 21st century, we would have to fly or sail across the ocean spaces

THERE WERE NO FLOWERING PLANTS OR BROAD-LEAVED TREES IN THE TRIASSIC, BUT THERE WERE PLENTY OF HORSETAILS, FERNS, CONIFERS, AND PALM-LIKE PLANTS.

in between. But in Triassic times we could walk there, if we had enough time and energy. All the landmasses are united as a single giant supercontinent, called Pangaea. Pangaea is so vast that most places in the interior are a long way from the moisture and cooling influences of the sea, so they are fiercely hot and dry. But don't worry, we won't even contemplate such an arduous journey – we'll stick to places that are less hostile.

THE TRIASSIC GLOBE. THE TETHYS SEA, A BRANCH OF THE OCEAN PANTHALASSA WOULD LATER SPLIT PANGAEA IN TWO.

By the seaside

The air is both moist and cool by the sea, but you know that over the dusty hills you can see inland there are vast swathes of

CYCADS ARE
SQUAT PLANTS
LIKE PALMS.

arid desert.
Huge waves
pound against
the beach.
They have had
a long distance
to travel across
Panthalassa – that's what we
call the vast ocean that covers
the rest of the Earth's surface.
Great for surfing!

At your feet, the tide-line
consists of shells that you have
never seen before. These are
mostly coiled ammonite shells,
whose empty chambers once
held octopus-like marine
animals. The tangle of seaweed
looks pretty much the same as
that from your own time.

and cycads. They
must have come
from a river that
empties into the
sea somewhere
close by.

Don't touch dead things

What's that smell? In the
distance lies the body of a giant
ichthyosaur, like a beached
whale. Long-tailed pterosaurs
wheel around it and squabble
over the decaying flesh.
Lobster-like creatures scuttle
over the corpse. The stench is
strong enough to convince you
not to go anywhere near that
nasty mess. Leave them to their
feast. You have come here
because you
want

Among the seaweed are
washed-up tree branches,
mostly from conifers, ginkgoes,

to see dinosaurs, so let's go
inland and do some exploring.

WEIRD WORLD

IN OUR TIMES, BIG ANIMALS TEND
TO LIVE LONGER LIVES. SOME
SCIENTISTS SUGGEST THAT
TYRANNOSAURUS MAY HAVE LIVED
FOR 100 YEARS, AND THE
BIGGEST SAUROPODS UP TO 200.

River safari

We walk up the bank of a river.
Here, where there is moisture,
there is also plenty of life.
Conifers line the riverbanks,
their roots in an undergrowth
of ferns and mosses. Between
the tree-trunks we see the
desert spreading away to the
horizon. There's a rustle in

the undergrowth, and a little animal scampers away. A dinosaur? No, it is furry and has whiskers and little ears, like a mouse. It is one of the first mammals.

small body, long hind limbs, balancing tail, long jaws, and sharp teeth. It is probably *Herrerasaurus*, one of the earliest known dinosaurs.

Our first dinosaur

Suddenly there's a lunge and a snap! Something snatches the mammal from the ground and shakes it to death. We can see the culprit clearly – it's our first dinosaur! The dinosaurs and the mammals have both recently evolved,

Giant newts

Upstream we go. The vegetation on either side is getting thinner as the desert encroaches. In the backwaters and swamps we see the murky waters swirl. Aquatic dinosaurs? You know better than that! There were no aquatic dinosaurs. These are giant amphibians, like newts as big as alligators. The time of large amphibians is almost past, but there are still plenty of them here. They seem to be settling into the mud as if they are preparing to weather out some dry times ahead.

but it's clear from this encounter which is the more powerful. The dinosaur turns and runs off between the trees, carrying its limp prey. We note the dinosaur's

HERRERASAURUS WAS A PRIMITIVE MEAT-EATING DINOSAUR, ABOUT 3 M (10 FT) TALL. IT HAD A SLENDER BODY, NARROW JAWS, AND POWERFUL BACK LEGS.

A pack of mischief

There is movement beyond the ferns. We push through the fronds to see a whole pack of *Coelophysis* scampering about, dipping their snouts between the ferns to snap up insects and snails. *Coelophysis* are very long, maybe as long as a family car, but most of the length is tail and neck. In body size they are no bigger than modern turkeys. Their forage path leads them away from the river to the sandy plain with its scattered clumps of fern. The season is changing and there is not enough food to be found beside the river.

A hungry journey

For days they trek across the wilderness, instinctively knowing the direction in which food lies. Now and again they trek across a drying pond, leaving three-toed footprints that will be fossilized in desert sandstone. The ferns become scarcer, and each clump that the pack finds is ripped apart for any insects that it may hide. But small stuff like this will not satisfy their hunger.

Eventually they reach a valley, where a drying river winds its muddy way through stunted trees. A group of bigger animals lives here. From their massive bodies and long necks we recognize them as prosauropods, probably *Plateosaurus*.

Food at last! Have you ever seen a healthy elephant attacked by a tiger? No. And you never will. There's something about really big animals that deters even the fiercest predators. These *Plateosaurus* are big, too, which is why the *Coelophysis* leave them alone. Suddenly there's a frantic bellowing nearby. An enfeebled old *Plateosaurus* is stuck in the mud-flats and can't get out. This is more like it – a plant-eater in trouble! Instantly the *Coelophysis* pack sets upon the hapless beast. Tearing at its long throat and tall flanks, they soon bring down the defenceless animal. Let's not look, it will be too horrible. That prosauropod is history – or even prehistory! But the *Coelophysis* will have meat for many a day.

COELOPHYSIS WERE SLIM, AGILE PACK ANIMALS THAT WERE BUILT FOR SPEED. WHEN FOOD WAS SCARCE THEY SOMETIMES HAD TO EAT THEIR OWN YOUNG.

JURASSIC JAUNT

We are scuba diving…in the Jurassic sea! Although it is more than 150 million years ago, under the waves we see the same white sand and the same clear blue water that we see off the Bahamas in our own time. We are swimming in one of the shallow seas that is spreading over low-lying areas as Pangaea begins to break up.

IN THE JURASSIC, THE SUPERCONTINENT OF PANGAEA BEGAN TO SPLIT INTO FRAGMENTS THAT SLOWLY DRIFTED APART.

PANGAEA

TETHYS SEA

PANTHALASSA

vanish into the distance. They must have been belemnites. Disc-shaped ammonites drift around more sedately, their big eyes looking out for prey. They are ignoring us – we're far too big for them.

A warm dip in the ocean
The main difference we notice is in the shoals of swimming animals around us. Unfamiliar fish nibble on the coral growing through the sand. Bullet-shaped things that look like squid weave past us and

PLESIOSAURS PROPELLED THEMSELVES GRACEFULLY THROUGH THE WATER, WITH SLOW BEATS OF THEIR HUGE FLIPPERS.

Jurassic jaws
What's that dark shadow passing over us? It's an ichthyosaur on the prowl. It is a smaller, more streamlined ichthyosaur than the whale-like creature we saw washed up on the Triassic beach. The ammonites draw in their tentacles and, with a

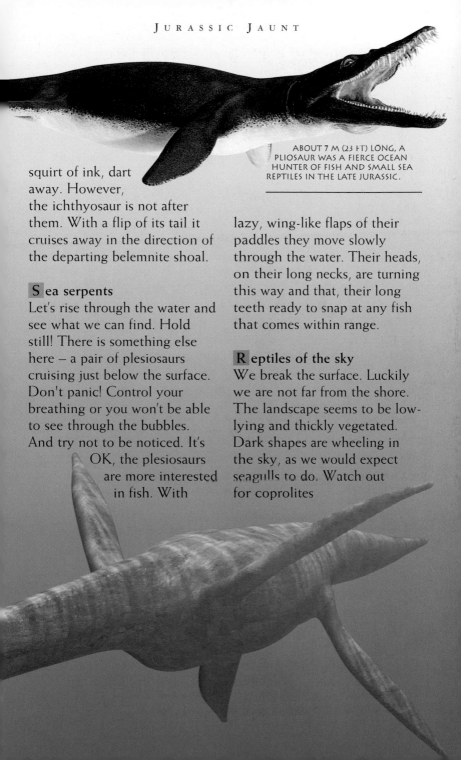

ABOUT 7 M (23 FT) LONG, A PLIOSAUR WAS A FIERCE OCEAN HUNTER OF FISH AND SMALL SEA REPTILES IN THE LATE JURASSIC.

squirt of ink, dart away. However, the ichthyosaur is not after them. With a flip of its tail it cruises away in the direction of the departing belemnite shoal.

Sea serpents

Let's rise through the water and see what we can find. Hold still! There is something else here – a pair of plesiosaurs cruising just below the surface. Don't panic! Control your breathing or you won't be able to see through the bubbles. And try not to be noticed. It's OK, the plesiosaurs are more interested in fish. With lazy, wing-like flaps of their paddles they move slowly through the water. Their heads, on their long necks, are turning this way and that, their long teeth ready to snap at any fish that comes within range.

Reptiles of the sky

We break the surface. Luckily we are not far from the shore. The landscape seems to be low-lying and thickly vegetated. Dark shapes are wheeling in the sky, as we would expect seagulls to do. Watch out for coprolites dropping from the sky! But these are not seagulls. Their big heads and leathery wings show them to be pterosaurs. We can spot both long-tailed and short-tailed types. Perhaps there are no birds at this time?

undergrowth and flaps clumsily towards the low-hanging branches of a conifer tree. It is *Archaeopteryx*, the first bird. It settles on a branch on all fours – it has claws on its "hands" as well as its feet – because it is

ARCHAEOPTERYX PROBABLY ONLY MADE SHORT GLIDING FLIGHTS

B eachcombers
On the beach we see a little chicken-sized dinosaur scampering along the sand, pursuing a lizard. It must be *Compsognathus*, because

not very good at perching. The flustered *Archaeopteryx* screams loudly at the reptiles in the undergrowth. So there are birds here after all!

that's the smallest Jurassic dinosaur we know of. The lizard weaves and dodges up the beach, disappearing beneath the arching fronds of the ferny undergrowth. The *Compsognathus* gives chase. Suddenly a dreadful squawking erupts from the foliage. A feathered form leaps disturbed from the

AGILE AND QUICK-FOOTED, COMPSOGNATHUS ATE CREATURES SUCH AS SNAILS, LIZARDS, INSECTS, AND FROGS.

G reen landscape
Ready to go into the forest? It could be dangerous. The vegetation, as in the Triassic, consists of conifer and ginkgo trees and cycads,

ARCHAEOPTERYX WAS A PRIMITIVE BIRD WITH TEETH, A BONY TAIL, WEAK FLAPPING MUSCLES, AND CLAWS ON ITS WINGS.

with an undergrowth of horsetails and ferns. However, there seems to be so much more of it. The air is much moister than it was during the dry Triassic, and the land is much greener. The oceans that are creeping in along the deep valleys formed by the splitting of Pangaea, and the shallow seas that are spreading over the land, are producing wetter climates. In fact, it is beginning to rain.

The forest browsers

Pushing onwards through the wet forest, knee-high in sodden ferns and with dripping boughs splashing cold drops on our heads, we suddenly find ourselves in an open clearing. A herd of huge beasts stands at one end of the clearing, their long necks reaching about like vacuum-cleaner hoses to munch the undergrowth as they go. The clearing is caused by them ripping up the vegetation. They are obviously sauropods of some kind, probably *Barosaurus* or one of the other long, low types.

There are about a dozen *Barosaurus* in the herd. Now and again, they reach up to scrape needles from one of the conifer trees. Their teeth seem to be designed to feed both high and

61

LOG ON...
www.dinosaurs.eb.com
is all about discovering dinos

THE HOSTILE DESERTS BEGAN TO DISAPPEAR
DURING THE JURASSIC, BUT THE CLIMATE
WAS STILL WARMER THAN IT IS TODAY.

low. They have heard us. One,
obviously the leader of the
herd, utters a loud steam-
whistle hiss. They all look up,
raising their little heads on
their long necks. Then they
troop off, following their leader
out across a shallow, rain-
dappled river. The soil of the
riverbank is trampled and
churned underfoot. In millions
of years' time, the rocks formed
here will not have the crisp,
well-defined layers that
geologists would normally
expect to

find in rocks formed
from river sediments.
Instead, they will be all
stirred up and mixed by the
messy *Barosaurus* footprints –
"bioturbation" is the fancy
name that geologists give
to this action.

As the *Barosaurus* cross the
river, the youngsters huddle
together for safety in the
middle of the herd between the
big adults. The nervousness of

such huge
beasts and
the defensive
structure of the
herd remind us that
this is actually a very
dangerous place and
time. There must be some
pretty big meat-eaters around.
We don't want to draw
attention to ourselves, so we'd
better tread carefully and try
not to make too much noise.

T rouble!
Keeping an eye open for big
theropods such as *Allosaurus*, or
even medium-sized theropods
like *Marshosaurus*, or small
theropods such as *Ornitholestes*,
we continue our exploration of
the forest. But, just our luck, it
is one of the big ones that
spots us. An *Allosaurus*
emerges from behind a
tree and notices us the

DILOPHOSAURUS, OF THE
EARLY JURASSIC, WAS ONE
OF THE FIRST LARGE
THEROPODS. THE CREST
ON ITS HEAD WAS
PROBABLY USED TO
ATTRACT MATES.

63

DINOSAURS

ALLOSAURUS WAS ABOUT 11 M (36 FT)
LONG. IT PREFERRED TO AMBUSH PREY,
BUT WOULD GIVE CHASE IF
NECESSARY.

A welcome diversion
Suddenly we find ourselves
in more open country. The
forested areas are separated by
large areas of more open
ground. And there in
front of us, swinging its
tail leisurely and casting
shadows with the broad,
diamond-shaped plates on
its back, stands a *Stegosaurus*.
The plated plant-eater seems to
prefer the more open spaces to
the confined forests. Out in the
open, its plates will not become
entangled in branches and the
wind can keep its enormous
body cool.

The *Allosaurus* plunges out
of the greenery behind us and
halts abruptly, distracted by
the plated dinosaur. We do
not expect the *Stegosaurus* to run

very moment we notice it.
Before long, its little brain
registers that we are potential
food. With a bellow it opens
its wicked mouth and charges.
Run! We take to our heels,
dodging around tree-trunks
to try to shake off our blood-
thirsty pursuer. We start to
panic as we realize just how fast
this large animal can run – it's
gaining on us!

away. Look at those hind legs. The thigh is longer than the shin. This is the sign of a slow-moving animal, because such a leg is not built for speed. It is an animal that will stand its ground. We expect a fight, but we are disappointed. The *Allosaurus* turns and stalks back into the greenery. It's more interested in picking off a young or sickly *Barosaurus* from the herd than staying here and tussling with the *Stegosaurus*.

That was a lucky escape for us. As the sun goes down over the Jurassic landscape, silhouetting a herd of *Brachiosaurus* against the fading light, we realize that this is no place for humans.

ALLOSAURUS WOULD SELDOM ATTACK AN ADULT BRACHIOSAURUS WEIGHING AROUND 70 TONNES, BUT ITS YOUNG WERE SOMETIMES A TARGET.

CRETACEOUS CROSSING

Now we are white-water rafting in the highlands of late Cretaceous North America, about 70 million years ago. We can call places by modern names, because Pangaea has broken up into the individual continents, which are slowly drifting into their familiar positions.

Rafting in the Rockies

The current carries us down the mountain river at breakneck speed. These mountains are the young Rockies, thrust up as the continent of North America pushes westwards against the floor of the

FLOWERING PLANTS BEGAN TO TAKE OVER FROM FERNS, HORSETAILS, AND CYCADS. THERE WERE MODERN-LOOKING CONIFERS AND BROAD-LEAVED TREES.

Pacific Ocean, wrinkling up the rocks along the edge as it goes. The rocks are sediments laid down in Triassic and Jurassic times – we can see fossils of *Coelophysis* footprints and ichthyosaur bones in the crags that rise around us. Up here in the windy heights there are few animals to be seen. The dark shapes of giant pterosaurs swoop around the cloudy peaks in the distance. These are pterodactyloids, the short-tailed type of pterosaur (the long-tailed types, the rhamphorhynchoids, have all died out by now). But the flying things in the mountain bushes nearby are all birds.

AS THE CONTINENTS DRIFTED APART, THE WORLD STARTED TO TAKE ON A MORE FAMILIAR SHAPE TO MODERN EYES.

Mountain vegetation

The torrent carries us onwards, through the gorges, over rapids, and down towards the foothills. The current eases as we drift along. Stands of conifers with a ferny undergrowth line the banks.

AN ANKYLOSAUR'S WEAK SPOT WAS ITS SOFT, UNPROTECTED BELLY

STEGOCERAS WAS A DOME-HEADED DINOSAUR LIKE PACHYCEPHALOSAURUS. RIVAL MALES MAY HAVE SETTLED DISPUTES OVER FEMALES OR TERRITORY BY BUTTING ONE ANOTHER WITH THEIR DOMED SKULLS.

Beasts ahoy!

We round a corner and come across our first big animals. On the inside of the river bend, where some flat rocks form a partly submerged shelf, two dome-headed *Pachycephalosaurus* drink from the water. They are startled to see us and quickly disappear into the forest.

Where they vanished, a broad armoured back can be seen rising above the ferns. An ankylosaur of some kind pushes through the undergrowth, its head down as it feeds from the low-growing plants. As we pass by, we see that it is one of the side-spiked ankylosaurs, like *Edmontonia*. However, it is difficult to see the exact arrangement of armour, so we cannot be sure of its identity.

This all makes sense. The most common fossils from bone-headed dinosaurs are of the solid skulls, and these are usually badly worn as though they had been washed downstream for a long distance. This suggests that they lived in upland areas. Likewise, ankylosaur armour is often found upside down, as if the dead body had floated

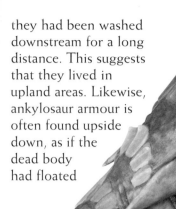

downstream and turned over as it decayed. This is the mountain life of the Cretaceous Period.

Modern plants

Now the vegetation begins to change. As we float farther downstream, the plant life becomes more colourful. The undergrowth now consists of little yellow flowers that resemble buttercups. Bushes with big blooms like magnolias line the banks. The primitive conifers of the higher slopes are now replaced by trees that look like willows and oaks. We could almost be looking at the vegetation of our own time, but something seems to be missing and we cannot tell what that is.

Plains migrants

Before long, the river leaves the forests of the hills and meanders over a lowland plain. Here the vegetation is of cycads and ferns – back to what it was like in Triassic and Jurassic times. *Pachyrhinosaurus* and other

MAGNOLIA IS A SURVIVOR FROM CRETACEOUS TIMES, WHEN FLOWERING SPECIES BECAME THE DOMINANT PLANT GROUP.

MIGRATING PACHYRHINOSAURUS MAY
HAVE TRUDGED 50 KM (31 MILES) A DAY.

horned dinosaurs of the
ceratopsian group live here. We
spy herds of them following us
down the stream. This does not
surprise us – in our own time
we have seen pictures of herds
of plant-eating animals, such as
buffalo or wildebeest, migrating
across plains. Here the situation
must be the same. The herds
move from one area to another,
depending on the season and
where there is food to be had.

WEIRD WORLD
FOSSIL SAUROPOD BONES WERE
ONCE USED AS BUILDING BRICKS. A
CABIN IN COLORADO, USA, WAS
BUILT FROM THESE FOSSILS BY A
SHEPHERD, BEFORE ANYONE KNEW
WHAT THE "BRICKS" REALLY WERE!

A watery grave
We notice well-trodden banks
where the ceratopsian herds
have been scrambling through
mud to cross the
river. There
must be
many disasters
as herds are caught
and washed away in
flash floods. You can just
imagine the panic and
struggle as terrified animals
trample and crush one
another, and the crocodiles
wait patiently for the losers.

In the distance, among some
cycads, we can see the long
necks of a couple of sauropods.
Most of the sauropods have
gone by now, being largely
Jurassic beasts, but there are
still a few left. And these
seem to be restricted to the
areas where the Jurassic-type
vegetation of primitive conifers
and cycads still exists.

A refuge

The current slows and plants close in around us. Instead of paddling down a broad river we are now drifting in a swamp. The river seems to have lost its course as it flows between the trunks of swamp trees and becomes choked with floating weed. Big shapes can be seen in the water here. A herd of duck-billed dinosaurs, *Edmontosaurus*, wallows in the shallows. These are not usually aquatic animals. They must be searching for food here, or else they are trying to get away from some danger. Danger it is! This is the home of one of the biggest meat-eaters of all time – the mighty *Tyrannosaurus*.

Dangerous country

The raft is aground. There is no more current. We will have to wade ashore if we want to see anything else. There's not far to go before we see what it was that frightened the herd of

SALTASAURUS, OF THE LATE CRETACEOUS, WAS RELATIVELY SMALL FOR A SAUROPOD. IT HAD BONY PLATES AND NODULES SET INTO THE SKIN OF ITS BACK.

IN MOST DISPUTES OVER FOOD, THE WEAKER TYRANNOSAURUS WOULD BACK OFF. BUT IF FOOD WAS SCARCE, A FIERCE FIGHT COULD TAKE PLACE.

Edmontosaurus.
A big *Tyrannosaurus* is crouched over the body of a freshly killed duck-bill, tearing it apart. And as we watch, it is joined by another *Tyrannosaurus.*
A rival, or a mate?

Close combat

The first meat-eater snarls and growls at the newcomer, which keeps approaching. Now the first begins to gesture and bellow. It is not going to share its kill. The newcomer gets the message and, after a few half-hearted growls, it turns and stalks away through the forest. Would it be wise to follow this beast, to see where it goes?

Maybe not, but let's take the risk. We lose sight of it briefly, but suddenly there is an eruption of growls and hisses, and a crashing of vegetation. It seems to have got into a fight.

Teeth against horns

And what a fight it is! A *Triceratops*, the biggest and strongest of the ceratopsians, has wandered into the hunting ground of the *Tyrannosaurus*...a big mistake! The two are now circling one another, looking for an advantage. We look for a thick clump of grass to hide behind, but we cannot see one. Now we realize what is missing from Cretaceous vegetation. Despite the modern look to the plants, there is no grass at all. It will not evolve until long after the dinosaurs have died out. Suddenly, the landscape seems alien and threatening. We should leave. A scampering in the undergrowth shows where tiny mammals of this time – little different from the one we saw in the Triassic – still run and hide from the great reptiles. So the environment is not as familiar as we first thought – it is still the domain of the dinosaurs. Oh, and the fight? Well, which dinosaur do you think was the victor?

A CHARGING TRICERATOPS COULD DELIVER A FATAL WOUND TO THE BELLY OF ITS ENEMY WITH ITS THREE HORNS.

AND THEN THERE WERE NONE!

The dinosaurs were the most powerful and important animals on Earth for 160 million years (humans have only been around for a mere 2 million). But then they disappeared. No one can be sure why this happened – it is one of the great unsolved mysteries.

A long-standing puzzle

One clue to this mystery lies in the rocks. Late Cretaceous rocks are full of dinosaur fossils. However, the rocks of the early Tertiary Period (the period after the Cretaceous) have none. There is a sharp boundary between the two. Not only did the dinosaurs die out by the end of the Cretaceous, but a host of other things perished as well. Gone were the flying pterosaurs, the swimming ichthyosaurs and plesiosaurs. The ammonites and belemnites also died out, as did the majority of the fish.

Strangely enough, the birds lost more than three-quarters of their species, but they managed to recover and took over from the pterosaurs as the masters of the sky. Even the mammals suffered vast casualties, losing three-quarters of their marsupial species. Like the birds, the mammals survived. They went on to replace the dinosaurs as the dominant land animals. But what caused all this death and devastation?

A WELL-PRESERVED BELEMNITE FOSSIL. BELEMNITES WERE ONE OF THE MANY GROUPS OF INVERTEBRATES (ANIMALS WITHOUT BACKBONES) THAT DIED OUT ALONG WITH THE DINOSAURS.

Meteorite impact

Maybe the extinction of the dinosaurs, 65 million years ago, was a sudden event. Imagine that you are watching the skies. In an instant, everything is engulfed in a dazzling light as a vast meteorite blasts through the atmosphere and explodes just behind the horizon. A few seconds later, the shock wave pounds you to pieces where you stand. That is sudden!

If you are a few hundred kilometres away, the shock wave will take several minutes to reach you. If you are not killed instantly, you will be hammered by flying stones and branches. Red-hot fragments will rain down from the sky. Perhaps the impact of the meteorite throws up an enormous ocean wave that sweeps inland, destroying everything in its path.

WHAM! SHOCK WAVES RACE ACROSS THE GLOBE AS A GIANT METEORITE CRASHES INTO THE EARTH.

into the atmosphere will prevent much of the Sun's light and heat from reaching the Earth's surface. Over the next few months, all the plants will die. You will have no food. It will become cold. You will freeze to death – that is, if you have not already died of starvation. This nightmare scenario is not just guesswork – there is evidence to support the idea that a meteorite may have ended the dinosaurs' reign.

Even on the other side of the world you will not be safe. You may well survive the initial shock wave, feeling it like a distant earthquake, but dust, smoke, and steam thrown up

RINGS OF MOUNTAINS WOULD HAVE MARKED THE IMPACT SITE FOR SEVERAL MILLION YEARS AFTERWARDS.

E vidence of the impact

In rocks that were laid down at the very end of the Cretaceous Period there are traces of the element iridium. This element is not often found at the Earth's surface, and the most likely source is from a meteorite.

VAST OUTPOURINGS OF LAVA ARE USUALLY ACCOMPANIED BY GAS AND STEAM CLOUDS THAT CAN ALTER THE CLIMATE.

There is also a buried structure that may be a vast meteorite crater in the Yucatán peninsula, Mexico, which dates from about the right time. What's more, beds of debris apparently laid down by giant waves have been found in rocks from the southern USA. All of this suggests that a meteorite the size of a small city struck the Earth in the Caribbean region about 65 million years ago.

Lots of lava

On the other hand, much of this damage could have been caused by volcanoes. Half of India is made up of lava flows that erupted about 65 million years ago. Volcanic eruptions as intense as this would have thrown up dust, smoke, and steam that would have had just the same effect on the climate as the debris from a meteorite impact. The element iridium is found in volcanic debris, as well as in meteorite rocks, so that might explain the high

EVEN THE BEST FOSSILIZED DINOSAURS, SUCH AS THIS EDMONTOSAURUS , TELL US NOTHING ABOUT WHAT WIPED THEM OUT.

levels of iridium in sediments laid down at that time.

Climate and disease

Meteorites? Volcanoes? All very dramatic. But maybe the dinosaurs' demise was not so spectacular. If, after millions of years of settled climates, the climates became colder or hotter, or wetter or drier, the dinosaurs might not have been able to cope with the changes, and gradually died out. Climate change may have happened if the sea level rose or fell, or if small landmasses merged to become bigger landmasses.

Perhaps disease was the big killer. You don't go to school if you have flu because

you don't want anybody else to catch it. But if everyone at school has already had the flu, you don't worry too much, because they will now be immune to it. Now imagine you are a dinosaur, and changing sea levels mean that you are able to migrate to new lands and meet other dinosaurs. You will spread diseases among them – diseases to which you are immune. And they will give you their diseases as well. Whole dinosaur communities may have been wiped out like this at the end of the Cretaceous Period.

A regular event

Whatever happened to wipe out the dinosaurs and the other animals of the time, it was not so unusual. Mass extinctions of this scale have happened about five times in the Earth's history. Smaller mass-extinctions are more frequent. Think of all the animals that have become extinct in the last few hundred years – the dodo, the passenger pigeon, and the Tasmanian wolf, to name just a few. It is possible that we are living through a mass-extinction at the moment. Worrying, isn't it?

GREAT CLIMATE CHANGES – SUCH AS THE EARTH BECOMING HOTTER AND DRIER – MAY HAVE CAUSED THE DINOSAURS' DECLINE.

WEIRD WORLD
IF THE DINOSAURS HAD NOT BECOME EXTINCT, WE WOULD NOT BE HERE NOW. IT WAS THE DINOSAURS' DISAPPEARANCE THAT ALLOWED THE MAMMALS TO BECOME THE DOMINANT ANIMALS ON EARTH.

THE DINOSAUR'S CHANGING FACE

The first dinosaur pictures and models looked very different from the ones we see today. We may be tempted to laugh at these early efforts, but they weren't bad considering that dinosaur pioneers had just a few bones and teeth to go on. The rest had to be clever guesswork.

The first restoration

If somebody gave you, say, an eye and a toenail and asked you to draw the animal that they came from, you could draw a very strange beast indeed, or you could draw something that you knew. This is pretty much how the first discoverers of dinosaur remains had to work.

In the 1820s, Dr Gideon Mantell and his wife Mary discovered fossilized bones and teeth in the Cretaceous rocks of Sussex, in southern England. Mantell was a country doctor who studied fossils as a hobby. He knew that these were reptile bones, and the teeth were like giant versions of those found in the modern plant-eating iguana lizard. That was all he knew. It is hardly surprising then that his restoration looked like a giant iguana. And that is why he named the animal *Iguanodon*, meaning "iguana-toothed".

A name for the giant reptiles

Sir Richard Owen, the most famous British naturalist of his day, invented the name "dinosaur" in 1841. At that time, there had been only three dinosaurs found – the ornithopod *Iguanodon*,

AN IGUANA LIZARD – LIKENED TO A DINOSAUR BY EARLY PALAEONTOLOGISTS.

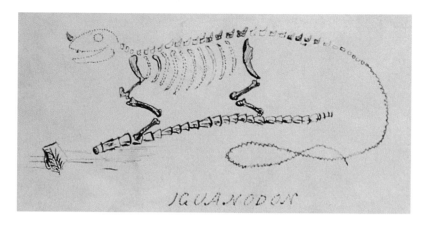

MANTELL'S FIRST SKETCH OF IGUANODON SHOWS A FOUR-FOOTED LIZARD.

the theropod *Megalosaurus*, and the ankylosaur *Hylaeosaurus*. (We still do not know a lot about that last one.) Soon it became like it is today – everyone was fascinated by dinosaurs and wanted to know more. When the Crystal Palace park was opened in London, England, in 1853, parts of the grounds were turned into the first dinosaur theme park. Concrete statues of all the dinosaurs known were set up, along with statues of the sea reptiles and pterosaurs. They are still there today – totally inaccurate, but beautifully

THE CRYSTAL PALACE STATUES REFLECT WONDERFULLY THE 19TH-CENTURY KNOWLEDGE OF DINOSAURS.

IF WE ONLY HAD THE SKULL OF A
RABBIT TO GO ON, WE WOULDN'T BE
ABLE TO TELL THAT WHEN IT WAS
ALIVE IT HAD CHUBBY CHEEKS, LONG
EARS, AND FUR.

atmospheric and excellent for understanding the state of knowledge at the time.

New discoveries

The first American finds were made in the 1850s, the best of which was the partial skeleton of a duck-billed *Hadrosaurus* found in New Jersey and described by Joseph Leidy, a professor of anatomy. The skeleton showed an animal whose hind legs were longer than its front ones, suggesting that it walked on two legs.

Then came an even better discovery. Over 30 *Iguanodon* skeletons were found in a Belgian mine in 1878, and most of those were complete and still joined together. Now people were getting a better idea of what dinosaurs were like.

Images based on evidence

A restoration is only as good as the evidence available. Imagine you had been given a pile of, let's say, rabbit skeletons, and most of those were still joined together. If you had never seen a rabbit and you were asked to draw a restoration of one based only on those skeletons, what would

A MODERN RECONSTRUCTION OF AN IGUANODON SHOWS AN ANIMAL WITH A HORIZONTAL BACKBONE. IT PROBABLY SPENT MOST OF ITS TIME ON ALL FOURS.

the result be? Probably you would not give it the rounded, furry cheeks that hide the big gnawing teeth. Certainly you would not know that it was supposed to have long ears. And what about the white cottontail? The picture you drew would be closer to a real rabbit than one

America, ornithopods such as *Iguanodon* and *Hadrosaurus* were shown as upright animals. And that is how things stayed for nearly 100 years.

I guanodon today
By the mid-20th century, scientists had learned more

MANY DINOSAURS ARE KNOWN FROM A SINGLE BONE

drawn from just an eye and a toenail, but it would still not be accurate. Based on the Belgian skeletons and the finds from

about how animals are built and the way that they interact with their environment. They could also apply engineering principles to dinosaur skeletons to show how

THIS EARLY RECONSTRUCTION OF IGUANODON SHOWED AN UPRIGHT ANIMAL SITTING ON ITS TAIL LIKE A KANGAROO.

they moved. Large ornithopods were now restored as four-footed animals that held their tails clear of the ground. They only rose on their hind legs now and again, but probably skittered around two-footedly as youngsters. Nowadays we can build what we are sure is a pretty accurate model of an *Iguanodon*. Look at the picture below. Yes, you've sussed it –

we've been using models throughout this book. We are luckier than Dr Mantell, nearly 200 years ago. We not only have a lot more knowledge about the lives and habits of animals of the past, but we can also use science and imagination to reconstruct the amazing world of the dinosaurs.

THIS RESTORATION OF IGUANODON MAY CHANGE AS NEW DISCOVERIES ARE MADE.

WEIRD WORLD
TO CELEBRATE THE COMPLETION OF THE CRYSTAL PALACE DINOSAURS, A SPECIAL NEW YEAR'S EVE DINNER WAS HELD – INSIDE THE HOLLOW CONCRETE MODEL OF *IGUANODON*!

REFERENCE SECTION

Whether you've finished reading *Dinosaurs*, or are turning to this section first, you'll find the information on the next eight pages really useful. Here are all the facts and figures, background details, meanings of dinosaur names, and unfamiliar words that you might need. There's also a list of website addresses – so, whether you want to surf the net or search out facts, these pages should turn you from an enthusiast into an expert.

DINOSAURS IN THIS BOOK

NAME OF DINOSAUR	MEANING OF NAME	WHEN IT LIVED (period/millions of years ago)	
Ankylosaurs			
Ankylosaurus	Stiff lizard	Cretaceous	70 mya
Edmontonia	From Edmonton	Cretaceous	73 mya
Euoplocephalus	Well-shielded head	Cretaceous	73 mya
Hylaeosaurus	Forest lizard	Cretaceous	125 mya
Nodosaurus	Knobbed lizard	Cretaceous	105 mya
Ceratopsians			
Pachyrhinosaurus	Thick nosed lizard	Cretaceous	70 mya
Protoceratops	First horned face	Cretaceous	80 mya
Psittacosaurus	Parrot lizard	Cretaceous	100 mya
Styracosaurus	Spear-spike lizard	Cretaceous	75 mya
Torosaurus	Perforated lizard	Cretaceous	68 mya
Triceratops	Three horned face	Cretaceous	66 mya
Ornithopods			
Brachylophosaurus	Short-crested lizard	Cretaceous	75 mya
Corythosaurus	Helmet lizard	Cretaceous	74 mya
Edmontosaurus	Lizard of Edmonton	Cretaceous	70 mya
Hadrosaurus	Sturdy lizard	Cretaceous	75 mya
Hypsilophodon	High-ridged tooth	Cretaceous	120 mya
Iguanodon	Iguana tooth	Cretaceous	120 mya
Maiasaura	Good mother lizard	Cretaceous	75 mya
Pachycephalosaurs			
Pachycephalosaurus	Thick headed lizard	Cretaceous	66 mya
Stegoceras	Roof horn	Jurassic	70 mya
Prosauropods			
Ammosaurus	Sand lizard	Jurassic	190 mya
Plateosaurus	Broad lizard	Triassic	220 mya

TIMELINE OF PERIODS AND ERAS

286 MILLION YEARS AGO	245 MILLION YEARS AGO	208 MILLION YEARS AGO
Permian Period	**Triassic Period**	**Jurassic Period**
Palaeozoic Era	Mesozoic Era	

Sauropods

Apatosaurus	Deceptive lizard	Jurassic	150 mya
Argentinosaurus	Lizard of Argentina	Cretaceous	93 mya
Barosaurus	Heavy lizard	Jurassic	150 mya
Brachiosaurus	Arm lizard	Jurassic	150 mya
Diplodocus	Double beam	Jurassic	150 mya
Hypselosaurus	High lizard	Cretaceous	71 mya
Saltasaurus	Salta lizard	Cretaceous	80 mya
Sauroposeidon	Poseidon's lizard	Cretaceous	115 mya
Seismosaurus	Earth-shaking lizard	Jurassic	150 mya

Stegosaurs

Kentrosaurus	Spiked lizard	Jurassic	152 mya
Stegosaurus	Roofed lizard	Jurassic	150 mya

Theropods

Albertosaurus	Lizard of Alberta	Cretaceous	72 mya
Allosaurus	Strange lizard	Jurassic	150 mya
Bambiraptor	Baby robber	Cretaceous	75 mya
Baryonyx	Heavy claw	Cretaceous	125 mya
Carnotaurus	Meat-eating bull	Cretaceous	100 mya
Coelophysis	Hollow form	Triassic	215 mya
Compsognathus	Pretty jaw	Jurassic	150 mya
Deinonychus	Terrible claw	Cretaceous	113 mya
Dilophosaurus	Double-crested lizard	Triassic	200 mya
Eoraptor	Dawn robber	Triassic	228 mya
Gallimimus	Chicken mimic	Cretaceous	73 mya
Giganotosaurus	Giant southern lizard	Cretaceous	83 mya
Herrerasaurus	Herrera's lizard	Triassic	228 mya
Marshosaurus	Marsh's lizard	Jurassic	150 mya
Megalosaurus	Big lizard	Jurassic,	165 mya
Ornitholestes	Bird stealer	Jurassic	150 mya
Ornithomimus	Bird mimic	Cretaceous	70 mya
Oviraptor	Egg robber	Cretaceous	80 mya
Suchomimus	Crocodile mimic	Cretaceous	120 mya
Troodon	Tearing tooth	Cretaceous	68 mya
Tyrannosaurus	Tyrant lizard	Cretaceous	65 mya
Utahraptor	Utah robber	Cretaceous	125 mya
Velociraptor	Fast robber	Cretaceous	80 mya

146 MILLION YEARS AGO	65 MILLION YEARS AGO	NOW
Cretaceous Period	**Tertiary & Quaternary Periods**	
Mesozoic Era	Cenozoic Era	

MILESTONES OF DISCOVERY

1822 James Parkinson, a doctor, gives the name *Megalosaurus* to a jawbone found in Oxfordshire, England

1824 Dean William Buckland, a clergyman, publishes a scientific description of *Megalosaurus* – the first serious study of a dinosaur.

1825 Dr. Gideon Mantell publishes a description of *Iguanodon*.

1837 Palaeontologist Hermann von Meyer publishes a description of *Plateosaurus*.

1842 Naturalist Sir Richard Owen invents the name "Dinosauria", later shortened to dinosaur.

1854 Life-sized dinosaur statues unveiled at Crystal Palace in London.

1856 Anatomist Joseph Leidy publishes a description of *Hadrosaurus*, the first North American discovery.

1859 The publication of Charles Darwin's book *The Origin of Species* puts the dinosaurs' development into an evolutionary context.

1860 First discovery of dinosaur-bird *Archaeopteryx* in Germany.

1870s & 1880s In the USA, fossil hunters Othniel Marsh and Edward Cope compete with one another for the best fossil discoveries. This bitter dispute becomes known as the "bone wars". About 150 new dinosaurs are discovered during this period.

1874 George Dawson discovers the first Canadian dinosaur.

1878 Over 30 *Iguanodon* skeletons are found in Belgium, giving a good idea of how dinosaurs were built.

1887 Palaeontologist Henry Seeley sets up the lizard-hip/bird-hip classification system.

1907–12 German expeditions unearth the first dinosaur skeletons in Africa.

1910–17 American and Canadian teams vie to find the best remains in Canada in a fossil "gold rush".

1922 American expeditions in the Gobi Desert led by Roy Chapman Andrews find the first undisputed dinosaur eggs in the Gobi desert.

1930s China is found to have many excellent dinosaur remains.

1938 Serious study of dinosaur footprints begins with R. T. Bird's discovery of fossil tracks in Texas.

1944 Allied bombing destroys valuable African specimens in Berlin, Germany, and also a dinosaur theme park, Hagenbeck's, in Hamburg.

1970s South America is found to be rich in dinosaur remains.

1969 John Ostrom suggests that dinosaurs were warm-blooded and gave rise to birds.

1974 Robert Bakker and Peter Galton argue that birds are dinosaurs.

1980 Dinosaur "bonebeds" are found in Canada, showing the mass death of a herd of horned dinosaurs.

1980 Luis and Walter Alvarez suggest that dinosaur extinction was due to a meteorite impact.

1980s Significant dinosaur discoveries are made in Australia.

1986 The first dinosaur discovery (an ankylosaur) is made in Antarctica.

1990s American expeditions to Madagascar find many important dinosaur remains.

1996 The first of many feathered dinosaurs is found in China.

DINOSAUR FAMILY TREE

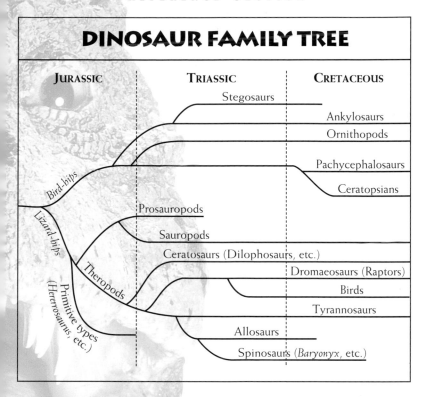

JURASSIC   TRIASSIC   CRETACEOUS

Stegosaurs

Ankylosaurs

Ornithopods

Pachycephalosaurs

Ceratopsians

Bird-hips

Lizard-hips

Prosauropods

Sauropods

Theropods

Ceratosaurs (Dilophosaurs, etc.)

Dromaeosaurs (Raptors)

Birds

Tyrannosaurs

Primitive types (Herrerosaurus, etc.)

Allosaurs

Spinosaurs (*Baryonyx*, etc.)

DINOSAUR WEBSITES

www.discovery.com/exp/fossilzone/fossilzone.html
Hear dino sounds, watch how dinos move, and build a dino from bones.

www.isgs.uluc.edu/dinos/dinos_home.html
Lot of excellent dino links at Dino Russ's Lair.

http://Ology.amnh.org/paleontology/index.html
Read interviews with dinosaurs, use an interactive dino family tree, and follow palaeontologists into the Gobi Desert on a fossil hunt.

www.nhm.ac.uk/
London's Natural History Museum has a "Dino Directory" and data files on all your favourite dinos.

www.nationalgeographic.com/features/96/dinoeggs/
Learn about dino mothers and babies, and hunt eggs with the experts.

DINO RECORDS

Longest dinosaur known
Seismosaurus, perhaps 50 m (164 ft).
Heaviest dinosaur known
Argentinosaurus, perhaps 100 tonnes.
Biggest predator
Giganotosaurus, perhaps 12.5 m
(41 ft) long and weighing 8 tonnes.
Smallest complete dinosaur known
Compsognathus, about 1 m (40 in) long.
Most intelligent dinosaur known
Troodon, with the largest
brain-to-body size

Dumbest dinosaur known
Apatosaurus, with the smallest brain-to-body size
Fastest runner
Gallimimus, about 80 kmh (50 mph).
First dinosaur in space
Coelophysis – a fossil was taken up in
the Space Shuttle in 1998!
**[These figures only refer to the
dinosaurs we know, and we think
that we know only about one-fifth
of the dinosaurs that existed.]**

SCIENTIFIC STUDIES

**The two main sciences involved
in the study of dinosaurs are
geology (the study of the earth)
and biology (the study of life).
Within these sciences are all
manner of other studies…**

Palaeontology   The study of
ancient life. Under this banner come
various studies, such as invertebrate
palaeontology and vertebrate
palaeontology, and also some
of the following terms.
Palaeozoology   The study
of ancient animal life.
Palaeobotany   The study
of ancient plant life.
Ichnology   The study of footprints
and other trace fossils
Taphonomy   The study of what
happens to dead organisms before
they become fossilized.
Stratigraphy   The study of the

layers of sedimentary rocks, the
sequence in which they were laid
down, and the conditions under
which they formed.
Palaeogeography   The study of the
ancient landforms – the positions of
the continents, the climates, and the
environmental conditions at different
periods of geological time.
Systematics   The study of the
diversity of organisms and their
relationships to one another.
Taxonomy   The practice of naming
different organisms on the basis of
their relationships.
Biogeography   The study of what
animals and plants are found in
different places, and why they
occur there.
Sedimentology   The study of
the formation of sediments and
sedimentary rocks, in which fossils
are found.

DINOSAUR GLOSSARY

Ammonite
A Mesozoic marine animal, like an octopus with a coiled shell.

Amphibian
Any vertebrate animal that spends its early stage in the water but its adult stage on land. Frogs, with their tadpoles, are modern amphibians.

Ankylosaur
An armoured, bird-hipped dinosaur.

Bed
A layer of sedimentary rock.

Belemnite
A Mesozoic marine animal, like a squid but with a hard, pencil-like shell.

Ceratopsian
A horned, bird-hipped dinosaur.

Coal
An organic sedimentary rock made up of fragments of plant material.

Conifer
A seed-bearing tree that reproduces by means of cones.

Coprolite
A fossilized animal dropping.

Cretaceous
The period of time lasting from 146 to 65 million years ago. The last of the three periods in the Mesozoic era.

Cycad
A primitive seed-bearing plant. Cycads look like palm trees, but are more closely related to conifers.

Diagenesis
The process by which sediments turn into sedimentary rock.

Duck-bill
A bird-hipped dinosaur with a duck-like beak.

Environment
The surroundings of an animal or plant – including the climate, the landscape, the altitude, the other animals, and the plants living there.

Erosion
The natural process whereby exposed rocks are broken down and worn away.

Flash flood
A sudden flood that sweeps down a river, following heavy rain upstream.

Fossil
The remains of a once-living thing preserved in rock.

Gastrolith
A stone swallowed by an animal to help in its digestion. In swimming animals, such as crocodiles, stones may be swallowed and used to adjust buoyancy.

Ginkgo
A type of tree with fan-shaped leaves.

Glass fibre
A tough building material consisting of hairs of glass embedded in resin.

Gizzard
Part of the digestive system of a bird, and some dinosaurs, that holds stones (gastroliths) used for grinding up food.

Horsetail
A primitive plant, related to ferns, that consists of a vertical stem with regular whorls of leaves.

Ichnology
The study of footprints.

Ichthyosaur
A fish-shaped marine reptile common in the Mesozoic Era.

Iguana
A modern-day plant-eating lizard from South and Central America.

Immune
Resistant to infection, unable to catch a disease.

Intestines
Tubes in the body through which food passes, and which absorb nutrients.

Invertebrate
An animal without a backbone.

Jurassic Period
The second period of the Mesozoic Era. The Jurassic lasted from 208 to 146 million years ago.

Laboratory
A place where scientific work is done.

Mace
A club-like ancient weapon that consisted of a heavy head at the end of a rigid shaft.

Mammal
A type of hairy, warm-blooded, vertebrate animal whose females produce milk and suckle their young. Humans are mammals.

Marsupial
A type of mammal whose females carry their young in a pouch on the body.

Mass-extinction
An event during which many different types of animal and plant die out.

Mesozoic
The era of history stretching from 245 to 65 million years ago and comprising the Triassic, Jurassic, and Cretaceous periods. The era preceding the Mesozoic was the Palaeozoic, when life began to move from the sea to the land. (All time before the Palaeozoic, when only very simple life existed, is called Precambrian.) The era following the Mesozoic was the Cenozoic, which includes the Age of Mammals and brings us up to the present day.

Meteorite
A piece of rock that has fallen to Earth from space.

Migrate
To travel from one area to another, usually in response to changing living conditions such as climate or the availability of food.

Mineral
An inorganic substance that is formed naturally by geological processes. Rocks are accumulations of minerals.

Mosasaur
A sea-living reptile from the Cretaceous period, closely related to modern monitor lizards.

Muscle
Elastic body tissue that produces movement.

Organic
Derived from or relating to living things.

Organism
A living thing.

Ornithopod
A bird-hipped, plant-eating dinosaur with feet like those of a bird.

Pachycephalosaur
A bird-hipped dinosaur with a very thick skull.

Palaeontologist
A scientist who uses fossil remains to study ancient animal and plant life.

Pangaea
The single supercontinent that existed during the Triassic period. It consisted of all the continents of the world fused together.

Panthalassa
The vast Triassic ocean that covered the part of the world not occupied by Pangaea.

Plesiosaur
A Mesozoic marine reptile with

either a long neck or a long head, and paddle-shaped limbs.

Predator
An animal that actively hunts other animals, known as prey, for food.

Preparator
A technician skilled in removing fossils from rock so that they can be studied by palaeontologists.

Prosauropod
A lizard-hipped dinosaur that existed in the Triassic and early Jurassic periods. It resembled a primitive type of sauropod.

Pterosaur
A flying reptile of the Mesozoic Era.

Pubis
One of the bones of the hip. In dinosaurs it either stuck forwards or was swept back. The classification of dinosaurs into bird- and lizard-hipped dinosaurs is based on the position of the pubis. In lizard-hipped dinosaurs the pubis pointed forwards, while in bird-hipped dinosaurs it pointed backwards.

Raptor
Strictly speaking, a bird of prey like an eagle or a falcon, but the word raptor has now become a popular term for a member of the group of theropod dinosaurs that had a killing claw on the hind foot.

Reconstruction
A skeleton of an extinct animal, built up from fossilized bones or casts made from the bones.

Restoration
A picture, film animation, or sculpture that shows how an extinct animal such as a dinosaur would have looked when it was alive.

Sandstone
A sedimentary rock made up of sand

grains squashed together and then cemented by mineral deposits.

Sauropod
A lizard-hipped dinosaur. Sauropods were huge plant-eaters that had long necks and walked on all-fours.

Scavenger
An animal that feeds from the bodies of animals that are already dead.

Sediment
Material, such as sand, mud, or silt, that is deposited on the bed of a river or the ocean. When this undergoes diagenesis it turns into sedimentary rock.

Shingle
Rounded stones that are deposited on a shoreline by waves and currents.

Stegosaur
A bird-hipped dinosaur with plates and spines on its back.

Supercontinent
A vast continent that consists of several continental landmasses fused together.

Taphonomy
The study of dead organisms before they become fossilized.

Tendon
The strap-like tissue that attaches muscle to bones.

Theropod
A two-footed, lizard-hipped dinosaur that had strong hind legs, long jaws, and sharp teeth. All meat-eating dinosaurs were theropods.

Triassic Period
The first period of the Mesozoic Era, from 245 to 208 million years ago.

Vertebrate
An animal that has a backbone. The backbone, or spine, is made up of many individual bones, each one of which is called a vertebra.

INDEX

CREDITS

Dorling Kindersley would like to thank:
Nomazwe Mandonko and Almudena Diaz for DTP assistance, Kate Humby for proofreading, and Chris Bernstein for compiling the index.

Additional photography by: Dave King, Andy Crawford, John Downes, Steve Gorton, Lynton Gardiner, Colin Keates, Harry Taylor, Jen and Des Bartlett and Gary Ombler.

Models made by: Roby Braun, Jonathan Hateley, and Gary Staab.

Picture Credits